Blessings to you!
We love you guys!

Jon
Prov. 3:5-6

Changing the Direction of Your Life One Day at a Time

TOM HUFTY

WESTBOW
PRESS®
A DIVISION OF THOMAS NELSON
& ZONDERVAN

WestBow Press books may be ordered through booksellers or by contacting:

WestBow Press
A Division of Thomas Nelson & Zondervan
1663 Liberty Drive
Bloomington, IN 47403
www.westbowpress.com
1 (866) 928-1240

ISBN: 978-1-5127-2790-6 (sc)
ISBN: 978-1-5127-2791-3 (hc)
ISBN: 978-1-5127-2789-0 (e)

Library of Congress Control Number: 2016901071

Print information available on the last page.

WestBow Press rev. date: 1/27/2016

Contents

Dedication

With indescribable love, I dedicate this book to my beautiful wife, Rhonda. There are no words that I can articulate that could adequately express how you have changed my life. Outside of Jesus no one has helped me make a *180* more than you. The words on these pages only reflect how God has used you to shape my life. Thanks for your love, your tweaks, and your patience. You help me love Jesus more every day.

Remember: it's you and me.

To Emmalyn, Kaylin, Vivian, and Pearl, my grand girls. You have captured my heart forever.

Acknowledgments

The pages you are about to read would not have developed without the help of several dedicated, loving, servant-minded people.

Thanks, Mackenzie, for bringing your desire for excellence to your edits and for loving me unconditionally. You're the perfect daughter.

Thanks, Zac, for your unwavering encouragement, undeserved admiration, and belief in and love for me. You're the perfect son.

Thanks to Sandra Rosenthal, my personal assistant, for your great attitude and daily efforts to make this work become a reality.

To all the staff, members, and attenders of First Baptist Church, Maryville, IL. I love you all.

Introduction

My dad was a true outdoorsman. Jack Chapple Hufty, born September 9, 1920, was raised on a dairy farm in northeast Missouri. He had Popeye-like forearms, the result of milking cows by hand twice a day for years. His biceps and legs were like chiseled rocks, the result of driving a team of horses to plow fields as a young man. In addition to dairy cows and row crops, the family farm consisted of hog, chicken, and cattle operations. Being the older of two sons, my dad had the responsibility to maintain all components of the family business. His dream? To be a major-league baseball player. His reality? Ninety-one years on the farm.

To supplement our family income, my dad became an electrician and commuted two hours each day to St. Louis to work as an electrical linesman. But his first priority was farming. During spring planting and fall harvest times, he would inform the crew foreman that he would not be coming into work for several weeks because no one was going to stop him from putting in or harvesting his crops.

In addition to instilling in me a strong work ethic, my dad passed on his love for hunting. To say that hunting was a passion of his would be an understatement. He was taught at a young age, by his father, to be a smart, trained, and conscientious hunter. He loved and respected nature and preferred to be outdoors. He hunted quail, deer, rabbit, squirrel, and raccoon. His skills were impeccable. We never went hungry.

I was his youngest. Born in the later years of my father's life, I never felt like he was too old for anything. He taught me how to play baseball. He coached my brother's and my baseball teams and spent countless hours teaching us the fundamentals of baseball. He instilled in me a love for the game. He also equipped us to be skilled hunters. My brother is a natural at it. Me? I'm okay. I think the best part of hunting was hanging out with my dad.

Even as a kid, I was impressed with my dad. He knew everything: farming, hunting, baseball—and God. He was a churchman and served his local church with as much intention as he tended to his work.

I took all my cues from my dad. Like I said, he knew everything. Throughout my life I have anchored many of my values and decisions on the lessons taught by and caught from my dad.

I loved what he loved.

On one special night we spent hunting in the back woods of our farm. It was one of the clearest nights I can remember. The sky was a phenomenal picture of deep blues and an overabundance of stars. Another great thing about living on a farm—we witnessed God's light show most every night. That night, it was just my dad and me. We had been walking through the woods with our hunting dogs for what seemed to be hours, with little success. I really didn't care. I was with my dad and I savored each moment of being outdoors, away from chores and homework. We kept walking through the woods, and then a strange thing happened.

My dad stopped, turned to me, and said, "I'm lost. I don't know where I am."

You can imagine what I was thinking. *Lost? You can't be lost. You grew up in these woods; these valleys and hills were your playground. You know these woods like the back of your hand. You can't be lost, because if you are lost, I am lost.* As my heart was pounding out of my chest, my dad looked up. He walked to a clearing in the woods and stared up at the starry sky. I wondered if he was praying. Was he trying to avoid looking at my wide-open eyes and fear-filled face?

Within seconds—but what felt like hours—he turned his eyes to me and said, "Got it," and began walking. I didn't say a word, but I followed.

After walking for about two hundred yards, my dad said, "This doesn't feel right." But he kept looking up and he kept walking.

"What doesn't feel right, Dad? If it doesn't feel right, let's go in another direction." He just kept walking. Within about thirty minutes, we found ourselves standing on a dirt road about five miles from home. Finally, he turned to bring me up to speed on his directional calculations.

"Son, when you are lost or don't know where you are, look up. I didn't know where we were, so I looked up and found the North Star. When I found the North Star, I followed it. As we walked, it just didn't feel right. I felt like I was going deeper into the woods and away from home, but I just kept following the North Star. It guided us to a familiar place. Remember: it may not feel right, but if you use it as your guide, along with the common sense God gave you, you can find your way out of a mess."

The rest of the journey home was silent. As we walked, many thoughts kept running through my head. *What did I just experience? How could my dad ever lose his way? I'm glad it's not cloudy tonight. I wonder if Mom saved some dinner for me.* Years later, I'm thinking different thoughts.

That experience changed my thinking. I took that experience and applied it to every aspect of my life. The life lesson my dad taught me was all about direction—the direction of my life. Making good decisions. Following the right people. Leading with humility. Looking up.

Some of us need a change of direction—maybe a U-turn, a reversal, or an about-face. Maybe you are lost and can't find your way out of a situation. Maybe you have come to the end of your own knowledge and need a spiritual turnaround. Look up. God is watching. He wants to guide you through this complicated life.

This book is about direction. It contains 180 thought-provoking devotions that can help correct a misdirected life. It is about gaining a healthy perspective in the key areas of our lives. The areas we need help with include attitude, character, faith, meaning, relationships, and service. Each of these areas is key to living a strong, significant life.

We all need direction. We all need guidance. Some of us need a 45-degree tweak or a simple reminder to get us back on the right track, whereas others need a full 180-degree turnaround. My hope is that the words upon the pages of this book will serve as a North Star to help shape your thoughts and give direction to the way you think, behave, and live your life. No matter where we are on our spiritual journey, we all need to look up, find our true north, and follow it.

Attitude

Your attitude shapes your life.

"Be careful how you think; your life is shaped
by your thoughts" (Proverbs 4:23 GNT).

Love First

Read
"Let love be your greatest aim" (1 Corinthians 14:1a TLB).

Reflect
She started it. I can't remember when she decided to do it. She does it every day—every morning, before the alarm goes off. Before we get vertical, she says it. Even if it is raining outside or we had an argument the night before, she does it. Even if the bank account is empty and the bill collectors are sending us scare letters, she says it. Every morning. Every day. They are the first words out of her mouth. My wife, Rhonda, with no one else but me in the room, says, "I love you." These are the first words I hear every morning. They shape my day. They have molded my life. There is no better way to start the day. She knows me. She knows every failure in my life. She knows every obnoxious pattern I need to change. She sees how gross I am as I grow older. She smells my morning breath, and that is not something pleasant. But she still says, "I love you" every day. Why?

Maybe it is because she knows I am going out into a wanting world that day, a world that wants my attention, and a world that wants me to fail. Maybe she knows there will be aggressive attempts to steal my joy that day, so she says it—first thing. It's like she is saying, "No matter where you are, what you are doing, whom you are with, or how life is going at that moment, remember that I love you."

I don't remember exactly when she started it; I just know she doesn't stop. I don't deserve it. She just decided to make it a habit. It's changed my life. I cannot shake it, nor do I want to. Those first words are powerful and have shaped my life.

Respond
Where did my wife learn to do that? In God's Word. When the Bible says, "Let love be your greatest aim," what does that look like? Rhonda figured it out. Start your day saying, "I love you" to the one closest to you. It is an attitude shaper, a life changer. She started it. Now I model it too. Because love works.

Remember
There is no better attitude shaper than demonstrated love.

Put On Your Dancing Shoes

Read

"'Let's have a feast and celebrate; For this son of mine was dead and is alive again; he was lost and is found.' So they began to celebrate" (Luke 15:23b-24).

Reflect

At the wedding of my daughter, Mackenzie, she said, "Daddy, I know you don't dance, but I want you to dance with me at our wedding reception." She didn't mean I had some big conviction against dancing. It's just that I don't dance. It's not an area in which I'm comfortable. I have two left feet and no rhythm—not to mention the fact that I was serving as a university professor and administrator at the time. In my line of work there are not a whole lot of dancing opportunities. I spent my days wearing suits and ties and attempting to appear dignified. But when your baby asks you to dance, you dance. So when the time came, we danced. Before it was over, I was leading a conga line around the room. It was like all this joy had been bottled up inside of me and was just waiting for an opportunity to be released at this wedding party. It was a blast that I will never forget.

Each story Jesus tells in Luke 15 ends with a party. This is what God is like. He demonstrates an attitude of celebration. He is a celebratory God. He is filled with joy when His children are close to Him. His nature is to throw a party when His children are reconciled with Him and each other. It breaks His heart when

His children fight or play the victim. That is not His way. His way is to connect with each other and celebrate (party).

Respond
The Bible reads, "No eye has seen, no ear has heard, and no mind has imagined what God has prepared for those who love Him" (1 Corinthians 2:9 NLT). Nothing compares to the joy that awaits us. For all of you wayward, wild prodigals who think you know how to party you have no idea. Your reconciling Father has a party planned in the future, and you are invited. Return home to Him. He is scanning the horizon, awaiting your return. If you know Him as your Father, the party of all parties is in your future. Don't miss it.

Remember
The Bible tells us that in the end there will be a party. So put on your dancing shoes and practice.

Changing

Read

"I tell you the truth, unless you change and become like little children, you will never enter the kingdom of heaven" (Matthew 18:3 NIV).

Reflect

Do you have someone in your life—a family member, friend, or colleague—whom you would like to change? I have noticed over the years that people will typically not change until they hurt enough, know enough, or receive enough. Pain speaks, knowledge speaks, and blessings speak. Sometimes I change when I have been hurt. Sometimes I change when I understand enough. Then there are times when I have an overwhelming sense of blessing in my life that compels me to change.

Changing is never easy, regardless of age. Notice that Jesus did not say to become childish but rather to become _like little children_. There is a big difference between the two. To become like a child means to take on innocence and dependence. The challenge set before us is not to acquire more knowledge of what it takes to be spiritual, but to humble ourselves to the point of obeying God, regardless of how that obedience affects us. On the other hand, to become childish means to live independently, always seeking to get one's own way. Which of these definitions best describes you?

Respond

Change begins with you. It is an act of the will. If a change in behavior is needed in your life, you must find the motivation that affects your mind and will. One motivator is God's Word. Scripture points you in the right direction. Prayer, when it is sincere, is another motivation to bring about change. It has been said that prayer changes things, but the truth of the matter is that prayer changes *me*. When I submit to Him in prayer, I see how great He is and how small I am. I see how His unlimited resources are available to me if I would just trust Him. I realize there are so many things that limit me but that nothing limits Him. Prayer changes my whole perspective of who I am when I ponder who He is. When you put the two together and pray what the Scripture says, it is a powerful motivation that brings purposeful change. When you pray His Word, it changes your attitude, which will change your outlook. A change in outlook, in turn, will change your life.

Remember

Authentic, lasting change begins within.

Cooperating with God

Read

"Listen to me, Asa, and all Judah and Benjamin: the Lord is with you when you are with Him. And if you seek Him, He will let you find Him; but if you forsake Him, He will forsake you" (2 Chronicles 15:2 NASB).

Reflect

One of the big words my children learned from watching PBS's *Sesame Street* was *cooperation*. The characters on the show would demonstrate in a childlike way how everything goes better when people cooperate. They would repeat their message over and over again, using catchy tunes I still find myself singing today. Come on, you remember: "Cooperation makes it happen. Cooperation—working together. Dig it." The goal was to teach children what it means to cooperate. O that the children of God could learn the same thing—not only to cooperate with one another but also—even more important—to cooperate with God. However, when we do not cooperate with God, it is evidenced in our relationships with others.

The prophet Azariah gave King Asa some sound advice regarding the character of God. We need to regard this as true for our daily lives. Notice: "The Lord is with you when you are with Him." Now we think the Lord is always with us—and that is true. His presence is with us always. But His blessing is only with us when we consistently seek to obey His will. God does not bless disobedience, but He rewards repentance (see Luke 15:11–32). Asa cooperated with God and cleaned out a whole nation (Judah) by destroying all idols.

Respond

Do you have an attitude of cooperation when it comes to God's will being worked out in your life? Have you been cooperating with God in your prayer life lately? Do you consult Him about all your involvements? He wants to be intimately involved in the details of your life. He longs for your cooperation so He can accomplish great things through you. If you're struggling with your cooperation level, tune into *Sesame Street* sometime. Become a child again and learn cooperation—with God. Dig it?

Remember

Cooperating with God leads to His blessing.

Crying about the Right Things

Read

"When I heard these things, I sat down and wept. For some days I mourned and fasted and prayed before the God in heaven" (Nehemiah 1:4 NIV).

Reflect

What hurts you enough to make you cry? What makes your heart ache even to the point of bringing tears to your eyes? For Nehemiah it was the news that God's once beautiful city was in ruins. The earthly representation of God's majesty was in disgrace, which made God look like a disgrace, and Nehemiah could not stand for that. When God hurt, so did Nehemiah, and the latter did not hide his emotion. He felt this news was significant enough to merit tears. But his sadness did not produce despair. On the contrary, his grief produced a determination not to allow the present circumstance to continue. He had what Bill Hybels referred to in his book *Holy Discontent* as a "Popeye moment," and in his heart he was thinking, *That's all I can stands, and I can't stands no more!* (Bill Hybels, *Holy Discontent* [Grand Rapids, MI: Zondervan, 2007], 230.

Something had to be done. The torn-down walls around Jerusalem must be rebuilt. After praying and fasting, Nehemiah put his faith into action. God brought about change and the walls were rebuilt, but He waited for someone (Nehemiah) who loved what He loved to join Him in the project. God still has projects He desires to accomplish, but He waits for us to embrace His heart, His direction, and His passion to accomplish the task. He could accomplish these tasks and projects by Himself. He does not need our help. But we need Him. So He waits for us to cooperate with Him. What a great opportunity we have before us, to cooperate with the God of all creation on His projects!

Respond
How few are the strong people today who cry over the evils of our present-day situation. It takes a strong person of great conviction to shed tears over the moral decay of our times. May God help us to see the world as He does, to hurt over the things that bring Him sorrow, and to team up with Him to correct the wrong of the present with His desire for the future.

Remember
By embracing God's attitude about life, you can be used to fuel the change that He desires.

Fatigue

Read

"Come to me, all you who are weary and burdened, and I will give you rest. Take my yoke upon you and learn from me, for I am gentle and humble in heart, and you will find rest for your souls. For my yoke is easy and my burden is light" (Matthew 11:28–30 NIV).

Reflect

I think all of us get tired every day. As a young boy working on the farm, I, after a hard day of hauling hay, would say to my dad, "I'm tired." My dad would respond with a sarcastic line like, "What's it feel like when you get tired?" After all, he had worked harder right beside me. He had arisen before I had, didn't quit until after I did, and was much older than I, so I had no place to complain.

But that's often the response of the tired. Fatigue affects our attitude. We complain. We don't like our circumstances, so we start playing the victim to get people to feel sorry for us. Even though we are Christians and we profess we want to be like Jesus, we forget that He never complained and never played the role of a victim.

Tired people can sometimes say and do inappropriate things. We let the fatigue trump our attitude and emotions. We start thinking that whoever dares to cross us had better watch out. Then we might say any number of hurtful things just because we are tired. Jesus has an invitation for all of us who are tired: "Come to me." That's it. Pretty easy, isn't it? He compels us to get close to Him when we are worn out physically, mentally, emotionally, and spiritually. He knows that the remedy for fatigue is being near Him. He wants us to get close enough to Him to embrace His attitude. His thoughts, words, and practices can teach us how to replenish our strength. He gives us strength when we are worn out, and He gives us hope when we feel like giving up.

Respond
Can you identify the things that drain your energy? Take a look at your calendar, identify how you spend your days, and try to recognize the energy robbers in your life. After you have spotted those energy sappers, do what Jesus said: "Come to me." Approach Him, and let Him lift your burdens.

Remember
God never grows tired of you. Never.

Happiness Is ...

"Watch out! Be on your guard against all kinds of greed; a man's life does not consist in the abundance of his possessions" (Luke 12:15 NIV).

Reflect

If someone asked you, "What are you waiting for to enjoy life?", how would you reply? Some would say, "When I get the things I've always wanted, I'll be happy." Others might say, "When I find that person who will fulfill my life, I'll be happy and satisfied." Then there are those who would say, "When I reach my goals, I'll achieve happiness and enjoy life." These are all noble quests, but none of them brings total happiness. So where does happiness come from, and how do you get it? Some people think happiness is found in an abundance of possessions. The latest toy, the trendiest gadget, or the newest whatever will not bring true happiness or value to your life. Some think that relationships will bring them happiness, but these people come to learn that people will fail you.

Notice how Jesus points out that joy in living is not found in gaining possessions of any kind. Getting more stuff or reaching some positional plateau will not bring you total happiness. You will not happen onto happiness when you reach a certain level of success. You will discover it when you choose it. Think of what James said: "Is your life full of difficulties and temptations? Then be happy, for when the way is rough, your patience has a chance to grow. So let it grow, and don't try to squirm out of your problems. For when your patience is finally in full bloom, then you will be ready for anything, strong in character, full and complete" (James 1:2–4 TLB).

Respond

Many people think that happiness will arrive someday: *Someday when I don't have to work. Someday when the kids are gone. Someday when I have a retirement home. Someday.* The problem is that *somedays* are dreams that may never come. Today is the day for you to be happy. You don't find happiness in a possession or a position. You find it in a person: Jesus. When you get to know Him personally, you discover happiness.

Happiness is for today. It isn't something you arrive at; it is an attitude you choose. It isn't just for weekends; it's for now—and it's for you.

Remember

Happiness is a choice one makes every day.

It's Party Time

Read

"I tell you that in the same way, there will be more rejoicing in heaven over one sinner who repents than over ninety-nine righteous persons who do not need to repent" (Luke 15:7 NIV).

Reflect

Are you into partying? God is! Not just partying to party, but partying for a reason. For God, changed lives are reasons to celebrate. God is into change. He created the four seasons, so He must enjoy the variety brought about by change. He makes leaves turn colors. He moves clouds across the sky and changes their shapes with His wind. But the change that produces a party in heaven involves someone's turning away from sin and toward Him.

Over the years I have been blessed to see God change lives. I have seen many people be moved by God's message to the point of repentance. They pivoted from their sinful patterns and then turned their life toward Him. One I distinctly remember spoke with my wife, Rhonda, after an outreach event we hosted. The young girl was so moved by what she sensed God was saying to her that she gave her life to Christ. She came up to me after she had talked with Rhonda and said, "I wanted to tell you that I've just given my life to Christ." I said, "Oh, that's great! You may not know this, but there are angels in heaven having a big party right now over your news." She smiled and said, "That's exactly what your wife just told me." (Great minds think alike!)

Would the attitude you have today fit in heaven? Heaven is a place of celebration when a life changes. Just imagine for a minute all of heaven breaking out into one gigantic party with your name in lights! You are the one making news in heaven; the place is going wild with joy! I don't know all that goes on at those parties, but I know they are parties like we have never seen.

Respond
In all three of Jesus's stories in Luke 15, He says a party was given. Why? Because a life was changed. God is into changing lives. Have you let Him change yours? Are you running away from Him right now, or are you running to Him?

Remember
If you know Jesus personally, there is a party in your future.

Leaving and Receiving

Read

"And everyone who has left houses or brothers or sisters or father or mother or children or farms for My name's sake, will receive many times as much, and will inherit eternal life" (Matthew 19:29 NASB).

Reflect

To be a consistent follower of Jesus Christ, you must engage in a "leaving." You must leave behind the things that were once the most important things in your life and then let Christ take their place. Now do not think this verse is saying that in order to be a real Christian you must disregard your family and possessions. The opposite is true. God gave you your family and possessions, and He expects you to be engaged with them. However, those gifts are never to become more important to you than the Giver.

The Giver, Jesus, is the one who brings contentment to our lives. Everything else is a cheap substitute. Our society promotes the idea that to find satisfaction we must constantly pursue something else that we do not have. Society says that contentment comes from external things. But the Bible offers us the exact opposite conclusion. It teaches that contentment comes when we stop striving for things. Contentment never comes from obtaining externals—*never!*

Respond

Do you have an attitude of contentment? Are you content with what you have, or do you have an obsession for more? Money can buy a lot of things, but it cannot buy the purity of true friends, genuine happiness, perfect health, or eternal life. That is why the Bible speaks so much about our attitude regarding money. God wants to protect us from messing up our lives or placing our security in the things that never satisfy.

Start your time alone with God by praising Him for knowing what is best for you. Then, thank Him for the blessings that follow your obedience to Him. Now, confess the times your eyes were not content with what God has given you. Finally, ask God to help you accomplish today what would please Him. Ask Him to help you *leave* the emptiness of striving for money and possessions and to *receive* the joy and contentment found in knowing Him personally.

Remember

Moving toward God means leaving the things that the world says are valuable. Embrace what He values today: love, truth, and relationships.

Looking for the Escape Route

Read

"No temptation has overtaken you except what is common to mankind. And God is faithful; he will not let you be tempted beyond what you can bear. But when you are tempted, he will also provide a way out so that you can endure it" (1 Corinthians 10:13 NIV).

Reflect

Whenever you work through a maze on a sheet of paper do you immediately start drawing a line without considering the route you are going to take? Or do you look over the maze first and then start your way through it? If you are wise, you probably study the maze in your mind before you actually start writing. Why? Because when you look ahead, you can see the traps. Not only that, you also can see the escape. Every temptation has traps, but God provides a way of escape. We must be faithful to look for it—and to take it.

What is your attitude toward temptation? The problem many of us face when experiencing temptation is that we refuse to take the escape when we see it. Our flesh enjoys playing with temptation so much that when we see the escape route, it frustrates us more than it encourages us. We want to play with the temptation a little longer. We miscalculate the danger and the damage that sin can bring to our lives. When we yield to sin, we get burned. Therefore, we need to develop a negative attitude toward temptation. We need to train our thoughts to hate it when we are tempted.

Respond
What temptation do you face most consistently? When you see the escape, are you encouraged or frustrated? If you are frustrated, your attitude toward sin is wrong. You need to develop a hatred for that sin; otherwise, it will destroy you. Go for the escape route and you'll experience freedom. Stay in the maze of temptation and you will be trapped.

As you pray today, praise and thank God for the escape routes He has made available to you. Ask Him to forgive you for the times you have seen His escape plan and refused to take it. Pray for strength to conquer the consistent temptation you face. Now go out and live in freedom today.

Remember
God gives us a simple instruction when facing temptation: *run!*

Make Yourself at Home

Read
"Let the word of Christ richly dwell within you" (Colossians 3:16 NASB).

Reflect
If I came to your house and knocked on your door, you probably would welcome me and say something like, "Come in. Make yourself at home." But if I started to move your furniture around to my liking, you probably would tell me to sit down and be quiet. Many times that is the way we treat God's Word. We invite Him into our lives and tell Him to make Himself at home. But when He starts rearranging our values, standards, and priorities, we put Him in the Sunday corner of our lives and say, "Stay there. I'll call You when I need You." But He is not interested in being a small part of your priority list. He is interested in taking over your priority list. He did not come to earth and die on the cross just to take second or third place in your life. He came to take over your life.

To let the Word of Christ dwell richly in you means that you develop an attitude toward His Word that permits Him to take over your life. The word *dwell* means, "to feel at home." God's Word feels at home in your life when you are transformed by it. However, many people today cannot honestly say that the Word of God dwells richly in them, because they don't make reading, studying, memorizing, or applying it a priority in their lives.

Respond

How much time during a day do you allow God to speak to you through His Word? He can speak to you in many ways, but when you know His Word, you can interpret much better when He is speaking to you through others or through circumstances.

If you want to be transformed today in your thinking and behavior, take some time to memorize some of His Word and look for ways to apply it to your daily life. The Bible was not given to us just for us to study it; we are also to apply its teachings. Sometimes allowing the Word of God to dwell richly in you is just a matter of cultivating organization and discipline. It's really not that hard. All you have to do is guard a time and place and then focus on Him. Ask Him to help you do that right now. Let God make Himself at home!

Remember

Prioritize time to spend with Him today.

Mirror vs. MRI

Read

"Your beauty should not come from outward adornment....
Instead, it should be that of your inner self, the unfading beauty
of a gentle and quiet spirit, which is of great worth in God's
sight" (1 Peter 3:3-4 NIV).

Reflect

Most of us have a love-hate relationship with mirrors. We are
not always happy with what we see reflected in the mirror,
but we sure appreciate getting an overall perspective and an
opportunity to make changes to our appearance before we walk
out the door. Wouldn't it be nice to have an attitude MRI so
we could see the reflection of our inner self? In such a case,
we might want to make some changes before we connect with
others. To make our lives count, we must be open to change—
genuine change that comes from within. Such change begins in
the mind. Anyone can make a few alterations or tweaks on the
outside and appear to be different, but on the inside a person
can still be caught up in the same old behavioral habits that have
been unproductive for years. But when we are willing to submit
to the authority of God's Word, real change can begin—and it
will be evidenced by a shift in attitude and direction.

Too often in our Christian life, the influence of the world
around us muddles our priorities. We tend to put more value
on acceptance than on integrity. We get distracted by the
beauty cult that surrounds us, and we emphasize external

beauty instead of internal character. The world says, "Image is everything." But image and outer beauty fade away, whereas character lasts and can impact others forever.

Respond
Peter said that a *gentle and quiet spirit* is what gets God's attention and approval. We should be exercising the disciplines that count in the eyes of God; then our lives will become productive for God's cause. When we cease trying to impress the world and instead focus our efforts on impacting the world, God is honored—and we are blessed beyond what the world can ever give us.

Stop and take some time to evaluate—it might be time for a change of attitude and direction. Make an honest assessment of your motives to discern why you are doing what you are doing. Then seek His direction for your life.

Remember
God looks upon the heart. What does He see when He scans yours?

New Wine

Read

"No, they pour new wine into new wineskins, and both are preserved" (Matthew 9:17 NIV).

Reflect

Do you know anyone who is legalistic? Legalism is a form of extremism. A legalist values the rules more than more than intent and definitely more than grace. In fact, legalism diminishes grace. Legalism is prideful and demands conformity to a standard. It exalts the person who keeps the law, which often leads to pride and arrogance. Legalism is manifested in false humility and boasting of what one does and does not do. It is focused on the individual and his or her measurement of good. It magnifies the law and minimizes a personal relationship with God. Jesus hated it. To Him legalism was a grace killer.

When Jesus spoke these words in Matthew 9:17, He was referring to the worn-out wineskin of Jewish religion, which centered on rules and regulations instead of on a relationship with God. The rules the religious leaders had made were legalistic instead of loving. Jesus was bringing a "new wine," a new way to worship that demanded a change on the part of the religious leaders. It required a change of attitude. But their minds were not open to change. When their comfort zone got the squeeze, they retaliated. They could not understand that the change would benefit them; therefore, they missed out on what He had for them—life.

Respond

New ideas are sometimes difficult to accept because they challenge us to get out of our comfort zone. However, if it were not for God giving us these opportunities to stretch, we would never be able to enjoy His promised abundant living. We would always settle for second best, and that is not desirable in God's sight. He desires for us to be all we can be. He wants more than anything to develop His mind-set in us. But if we are set in our ways and refuse to accept his guidance, it is like pouring new wine into old wineskins—they will burst and break apart.

Has your mind-set been aligned with Christ's, or do you have some old wineskins (attitudes) that need to be changed? Do you need to be stretched in your thinking of how God can use you? Determine to increase grace and to decrease legalism in your life.

Remember

Embrace the teachings of Jesus. Find opportunities to distribute grace.

"Oh No" vs. "Oh Wow"

Read

"Now Joseph had been taken down to Egypt. Potiphar, an Egyptian who was one of Pharaoh's officials, the captain of the guard, bought him from the Ishmaelites who had taken him there. The Lord was with Joseph" (Genesis 39:1–2a NIV).

Reflect

Here is a drama for you.

> "Hey, Joseph, your dad had twelve sons—and you are his favorite!"
> "Oh wow!"
> "But your brothers hate you and plan to sell you as a slave to get rid of you."
> "Oh no!"
> "But you will live in the home of the captain of the Guard and enjoy a privileged lifestyle."
> "Oh wow!"
> "But his wife will frame you, and you will be sent to prison."
> "Oh no!"

This drama continued for Joseph until he was thirty years old. His life was a series of "oh wows" and "oh nos." But that is not really that unusual, is it? We all encounter "oh wows" and "oh nos" in life. The problem comes when we choose to live our life in the "oh nos."

Joseph didn't look at things that way, because *the Lord was with Joseph*. When you are walking with the Lord, you have a different perspective than the world system does. Joseph even named his firstborn son Manasseh, which means "forgotten." In other words, "I choose to forget all the troubles I have encountered. Every time I see my son, I will be reminded that I will not live in the past, for I could become bitter." Joseph saw the danger of living in the "oh nos" of life and took measures to avoid them.

Respond

Do you live in the "oh wows" or in the "oh nos" of life? There are plenty of "oh wows"! Jesus came to earth to pay the penalty for your sin. Oh wow! He chose to take on the shame for your sin so you would not have to. Oh wow! He told you not to allow your heart to be troubled, as He would go and prepare a place for you in heaven. Oh wow! His Word says that the eye has not seen, the ear has not heard, and the mind cannot begin to comprehend what God has in store for those who love Him. Oh wow, oh wow, oh wow!

Remember

"Oh nos" are temporary. Trust God for His "oh wow" factor to be worked out in your life.

Persistence and Determination

Read

"So we rebuilt the wall till all of it reached half its height, for the people worked with all their heart" (Nehemiah 4:6 NIV).

Reflect

There is no rabbit's-foot methodology to success. Succeeding takes hard work and a lot of persistence and determination. Napoleon Hill studied the lives of many successful people: Thomas Edison and Henry Ford, to name two. He stated that as he studied these two extraordinary men, he found no quality, save persistence, that even remotely suggested the major source of their stupendous achievements (Napoleon Hill, *Think and Grow Rich* [New York: E. P. Dutton, Inc., 1958], 164).

I am afraid that, too often, we see things not as they are but as we are. We look at ourselves and where we came from and say, "Oh, I couldn't do that," when it is for that very purpose, for doing a specific task that God has placed us where He has. More often we fail not because we can't see His plan and perform it, but because we refuse to see it and are not willing to perform it. We lack the key ingredient—determination. What kind of determination? The kind of determination to follow through when we are ridiculed by the majority. The determination to stick to the job when others say, "We have never done it that way before."

God looks for people who will follow His plan and continue with the job at hand in a society and as part of a generation that is ruled by a throwaway lifestyle. Our generation throws away marriages, throws away children, and throws away family values like we throw away paper plates at a picnic. All the while God cries out for those who will hear His call to be persistent and to receive His blessing for showing continued faithfulness to His plans.

Respond
You may read these words and feel like you are a victim of this throwaway society. Let me assure you that God has not thrown you away. In fact, He wants you to play a part in His plans for the future. Can you trust Him enough to be determined in the face of opposition? Yes! It will take prayer, trust, and your greatest commitment. Will it be worth it? Ask Nehemiah (read Nehemiah 6:15–16).

Remember
God has a plan for your life today.

You Can

Read

"I can do all this through him who gives me strength"
(Philippians 4:13 NIV).

Reflect

Do you keep your promises? I am told there are 7,474 promises in God's Word. Every one of those promises from Him has been kept or will be kept. God is thrilled to show Himself faithful to what He says. These promises were made so we would believe them, act on them, and have our lives and spiritual walk affected by them. When we claim and believe His promises, He responds by blessing our faith.

For most believers, the problem is not accepting the promises of God. Instead, the problem is acting on His promises. There is a difference between accepting and acting. Accepting is passive. It's like saying, "I accept that there is air," but never acting on it by inhaling. When you do not act on what you accept, you will never experience the fullness of your belief. Every promise God gives us has a prerequisite to follow. When we obey the prerequisite, He fulfills His promise according to His perfect timing. Acting upon His promise is the precursor to amazing things happening.

Respond

The promise of Philippians 4:13 is, "I can do all things." The prerequisite is that I have to allow Him to give me the strength.

That means I do not ignore His gift and attempt to do things my way and on my own. Let's say He wants you to forgive someone for hurting you. You *can* forgive, but not in your own power, because more than likely, the person will hurt you again and you will just grow more angry and bitter. With His strength, you *can* make a decision to forgive and give up bitterness.

Perhaps God wants you to stop a bad habit you can't seem to shake. You know you need to stop it, but you justify continuing it almost daily. You *can* stop it, but not without His help. Seeking Him and asking Him for His strength can help you overcome the habit. You *can do all things* if you let Him strengthen you.

"Can't" is the mind-set of the wimpy Christian. If we seek to develop the attitude of Philippians 4:13, we will have His strength at our disposal—and victory over obstacles *can* become an everyday occurrence.

Remember
You can trust Him because He always keeps His promises.

Strengthening the Walls

Read

"Then I said to them, 'You see the trouble we are in: Jerusalem lies in ruins, and its gates have been burned with fire. Come, let us rebuild the wall of Jerusalem, and we will no longer be in disgrace'" (Nehemiah 2:17 NIV).

Reflect

How do you respond when you notice a problem? Many people have the ability to identify problems. In fact, our government spends a lot of dollars conducting studies to identify problems. But the mark of good leaders with positive attitudes is not that they are able to identify the problem (which is necessary), but that they can see the need, identify the problem, and work to bring a solution.

Sometimes when we see a need, the first thing we do is to search for someone to blame. Nehemiah, however, did not look for a scapegoat; instead, he took responsibility for the solution. Wasted time and energy are the results of passing the buck. But those who avoid such traps and who keep God's vision in focus are the ones who accomplish God's will in their lives. Blaming others also hinders motivation. No one wants to follow someone who always makes excuses.

So what motivated the people to follow Nehemiah? He gave them a reason to follow. The reason? "We will no longer be in disgrace." If we are going to fulfill God's dream for our lives, we must see the needs around us and within us, and then find and work the solution.

Respond
Walls around cities were built primarily for defensive purposes. In the same way, we should build walls around our lives to prevent us from being injured by the attacks of the world. These protective walls can be in the form of predetermined decisions not to associate with sinful people or be in sinful environments. Or we may choose to stay away from tenuous situations that could speak to our vulnerability and lead us to compromise our Christian values. If we keep our walls built up and strong, we can stand as a testimony of God's goodness.

How are the walls of your life? Have they been made strong by decisions to protect yourself? Are they strong, or are they disgraceful? Have you allowed foreign enemies inside the walls of your life? Do you see the need to strengthen the walls of protection around your life? Fortify your convictions with the truth of His Word.

Remember
Building walls around your life can keep you from disgrace.

The Attitude of Giving

Read

"But the earlier governors—those preceding me—placed a heavy burden on the people and took forty shekels of silver from them in addition to food and wine. Their assistants also lorded it over the people. But out of reverence for God I did not act like them" (Nehemiah 5:15 NIV).

Reflect

When "everybody else is doing it," watch out! Throughout history, the majority has been wrong several times. Nehemiah didn't make his decision based on the actions of his predecessors. He did not follow the flow of the crowd or the ones who said, "We have always done it this way." Instead, he based his actions on what God thought, because his goal was to honor God with his behavior. In this case, it meant that he had to avoid the attitude of entitlement that came with his position and to steer clear of the temptation to be greedy.

The opposite of greed is giving, and the opposite of entitlement is humility. Jesus is the best example of giving and humility that has ever walked on earth. He humbled Himself through obedience to the Father. Jesus also gave His life so that we can have eternal life. It is a gift we could not earn if we tried. Secondly, Jesus gave His Word. It is not enough that we receive His gift of eternal life. We must receive His Word daily in order to gain inner strength and cleansing for the inner person. God also gave us the Bible, His Word, as a gift of constant truth for us. All these gifts have an eternal nature. They are gifts that we enjoy, now and forever. Time and space do not allow us to consider all the material gifts He has given us, but we do know that every good and perfect gift comes to us from God our Father (James 1:17).

Respond
Now that you have considered just a sampling of how much God has given you, consider your attitude toward giving to others. It could be that you can offer the gift of a listening ear or an encouraging word. It may be that you can help someone financially in an anonymous way. Whatever way God may direct you, remember that to imitate Jesus means to be a giver.

Remember
Becoming a giver, as a habit of life, diminishes any inclination toward becoming greedy.

Serious Confession

Read

"Those of Israelite descent had separated themselves from all foreigners. They stood in their places and confessed their sins and the wickedness of their fathers. They stood where they were and read from the Book of the Law of the Lord their God for a quarter of the day, and spent another quarter in confession and in worshipping the Lord their God" (Nehemiah 9:2–3 NIV).

Reflect

I learned at a young age that if I would just admit it when I messed up, things would go better for me than if I denied my misbehavior or tried to justify it.

The people of God were seeking Him and trying to please Him like they never had before, and God was working in their midst. They spent half of the day engaging God and expressing their sorrow for their sin. God had captured their attention through His Word, and they responded in a way that pleased Him. They developed an attitude about their sin. They grew to hate it. They started agreeing with God about their sin, and this led to a closer relationship to Him.

After the Word of God was read by Ezra, it was determined that adjustments needed to be made in the lives of the people. Notice what the children of Israel did when they heard God's Word. They began by separating themselves from those who did not share their values. This is one of the first steps toward holiness, when you step away from the influences of the ungodly.

Then they stood in their places and confessed their sins. They did not go out and try to justify their sin to others. They dealt with their sin quickly by confessing it. They knew they needed forgiveness, and they sought it from God with an attitude of humility.

Respond
Nehemiah 9 contains the longest prayer in the Bible. The prayer reveals the complete repentance of the people and the utter confidence they had in God. After a lengthy period of thinking, meditating, and planning, they came to a conclusion. The conclusion was to strike up a contract that would be signed by the leaders indicating that they meant business about being obedient to God. How would you respond if you were asked to sign your name to an agreement that said you were serious about your obedience to God?

Remember
Confess and be blessed.

The Attitude of Humility

Read

"The first thing Andrew did was to find his brother Simon and tell him, 'We have found the Messiah' (that is, the Christ)" (John 1:41 NIV).

Reflect

The people in my life who have impressed me the most never tried to. Why? Because they were humble. They had a quiet, unassuming personal security about them that did not need the spotlight. They were just true to themselves, not trying to be or become someone they were never intended to be.

Andrew was that way. He has to be one of the most humble guys in the New Testament, for all through the gospels he is referred to as "Simon Peter's brother." It was never "Simon Peter, Andrew's brother." He was always following in his big brother's shadow. At the famous feeding of the five thousand, Andrew was referred to in the same way. Everyone knew Peter. He was the bold one, the extrovert with the powerful personality. Peter was the exuberant, boisterous disciple who naturally drew people to himself while Andrew faded into the background. Little brother Andrew was an easy-to-miss type of guy.

However, Andrew was not passive. Notice the first thing that Andrew did after finding the Messiah was to find his brother Simon and tell him about it. Two things were evident: (1) Andrew loved his brother, and (2) he knew he needed to get him to Jesus. Through this observation, we can learn from Andrew that when you really connect with Jesus, you naturally want others to connect to Him too.

Respond

The one who truly reaches out is the humble-hearted one who doesn't care so much about position or credit but who cares about people who need to know Jesus. Do you think Andrew ever got tired of hearing, "Oh, you're Simon Peter's brother"? Andrew was unencumbered by self, and he introduced his brother to Christ. Did Andrew ever complain? There are no records to indicate he did. He simply wanted his brother to know Jesus.

Position meant little to Andrew; all he wanted to do was to be a contagious Christian. In fact almost everywhere you see Andrew's name in Scripture, he is bringing someone to Jesus. O that we could be remembered that way!

Remember

"True humility and fear of the Lord lead to riches, honor, and long life" (Proverbs 22:4 NLT).

The Attitude of Loving

Read

"If you have any encouragement from being united with Christ, if any comfort from his love, if any fellowship with the Spirit, if any tenderness and compassion, then make my joy complete by being like-minded, having the same love, being one in spirit and purpose" (Philippians 2:1–2 NIV).

Reflect

How did you learn to love? The ability to love is not something we acquire automatically. Instead, we learn to love as it is modeled to us. The first modeling of mentoring love we receive usually comes from our parents. Depending on the life situation, a grandparent may be the model of love. But regardless of who the model is, if we are going to be a loving person as a matter of habit, then we need a model of love from whom to learn. In today's Scripture, Paul is trying to help us see that Christ is the true model of love. If we imitate Him, we are demonstrating authentic and real love.

However, attitudes must be practiced and developed because they are a discipline of the mind. For example, if you play on a team and expect to win, you must first think you are a winner before you even take the field to play. Success, winning, and achievement all start with the right attitude. In the same way, loving properly comes from the right attitude, the same attitude Christ had.

When you are involved in a relationship, whether business or social, your attitude will determine the length and quality of love you show in that relationship. If your attitude is conceited and prideful, chances are your relationship will be one-sided and shallow. Why? Because people have a tendency to distrust those who are self-absorbed. But when you take on the attitude of humility and the role of service in a relationship as Jesus did, a natural trust level will begin to develop. Your relationship will have the opportunity to grow and flourish.

Respond
Take some time right now to evaluate your love models. Measure them against the true love model of Christ. Take time to praise and thank Him for His love. Ask Him to reveal to you the times you have been selfish and prideful so you may confess them to Him. Practice demonstrating His kind of love to others today.

Remember
People are desperately seeking authentic love. You can be a model of Christ's love today.

The Morning News

Read

"They do not fear bad news; they confidently trust the Lord to care for them" (Psalm 112:7 NLT).

Reflect

"Breaking-news alert!" Most news channels announce a breaking-news alert about every ten minutes. They're saying, "You *must* listen." Hey, I have another news alert for you. You don't have to listen. Our world has news happening all the time, and usually the events have nothing to do with your personal life. In fact, when you become addicted to the news, you have invited one of the most negative mind molders into your life. The media makes their money on reporting, investigating and unfortunately sometimes making up the news. What happened to the good old days when news reports were just that—reports? News agencies didn't try to make the news (for ratings). They simply reported it.

I want to invite you to a fast—not one of food, sugar, or any of those things you often hear news alerts about concerning substances that will kill you if you eat enough of them. I want to invite you to a fast from the news. Read it once a day and give it ten minutes of your time. Then put it down, walk away from it, and live! You will be adequately informed, and you will have a better attitude about life, others, and yourself as a result.

Respond

The psalmist makes an indirect observation about bad news. He implies that bad news feeds fear. Fear is one of the things that weakens the courageous. It slows down, confuses, and alarms those who would be confident. It's the enemy of courage and the assailant of bravery. It intimidates security and robs a person of the positive. The psalmist said that those who embrace righteousness will not be shaken by bad news.

Why didn't David sit down and wring his hands in fear when he heard the "breaking-news alert" that a giant named Goliath was making threats against his people? Why didn't Daniel decide not to pray to the king when he heard the "breaking-news alert" that no one was allowed to pray to anyone but the king? Why didn't Nehemiah stop building when he heard the "breaking-news alert" that the wall he was constructing around Jerusalem would fall if a fox jumped on it? The answer is that each one of these men found his purpose and put his confidence in the Lord.

Remember

Trust triumphs. Fear fails.

The Right Attitude to Have When You Hurt

"Blessed are those who mourn, for they will be comforted" (Matthew 5:4 NIV).

Reflect
One of the most difficult times to have a good attitude is when something or someone has hurt you. It's tough because a host of feelings run through you: feelings of guilt (*What did I do wrong?*), feelings of revenge (*I want him to hurt as badly as I do*), or feelings of self-pity and loneliness.

Jesus felt each of those emotions. He knew firsthand what it was like to be mistreated and to feel the pain of loss and rejection. No person on earth has hurt any more than Jesus. He hurt emotionally, mentally, and physically while He was here on earth. No wonder he can say, "Blessed are those who mourn"—because He knew that pain was not an end in itself. One of the most remarkable things about Jesus is that despite all His suffering, nothing was ever recorded to indicate that He whined or complained. Nowhere in Scripture does it say that Jesus played the victim.

Jesus' promise to hurting people is that they will be comforted. The truth is that no one can heal a hurt the way Jesus can. He knows and fully understands our hurt. He has experienced the hurt this world can dish out. No one can share our feelings the way He can. Jesus may not choose to change what goes on around us, but He can change what goes on within us while we are going through difficult circumstances.

Respond

Are you hurting right now? Have you experienced rejection or loss recently? The first thing you need to remember is that you are not alone. Having a good attitude while you hurt is not something you "feel into action." Rather, it is something you act on—and then the feelings follow. Acting on something even when you don't feel like it is hard. But if you don't take that step, and if you don't choose to change the way you think about your situation, then you will be choosing to let your feelings take you down the road of self-pity. When you choose this road, you are allowing circumstances to control you—and victimization is right around the corner.

Remember

Take some time to share your hurts with God. Let Him comfort you like no one else can.

The Right Motives

Read

"Each man should give what he has decided in his heart to give, not reluctantly or under compulsion, for God loves a cheerful giver" (2 Corinthians 9:7 NIV).

Reflect

I find it very easy to give to my children when they demonstrate the proper attitudes toward others and me. However, when their attitudes become sour, my generosity quickly finds its limits. Now, don't get me wrong! I still love them like always. I still provide for them without question, but I will not reward a bad attitude.

Along the same line of thinking, giving money, time, or your gifts to the work of the Lord is a matter of the heart. Once you understand the benefits of giving with a cheerful attitude, it's foolish not to be a giver. In fact, giving will become a natural outcome of growth. It all starts in the heart. God is much more concerned about the attitude of your heart than He is about the amount of money in your back account.

Respond

Just as I find it difficult to reward my children when they have a rotten attitude, I find it enjoyable to reward them when they are demonstrating the right attitude. When they build each other up, share, and cheerfully contribute to the health of the family, it's a joy for me to reward them. In fact, you can't stop me from rewarding them. And guess what? It's the same way with God when we are cheerful givers.

Giving is a lot like love—it never diminishes us and only helps our spiritual situation. Therefore when we give, it should be with a cheerful attitude, because we know we will benefit just as those who receive the gift, if not more.

If you give because you feel you have to, it may be an indicator that you should evaluate your motives about giving. Take some time right now to praise and thank God for all He has given you. Be specific. Think about the tangible things and the intangibles He has graciously given you. Then pray and ask Him to forgive you for the times when you did not demonstrate the right motives in your giving. Ask Him to help you look at giving as a privilege. Now go out and be a cheerful giver today!

Remember
God examines our motives. Check yours today.

The Value of Tough Times

Read
"You intended to harm me, but God intended it for good to accomplish what is now being done, the saving of many lives" (Genesis 50:20).

Reflect
Children have a way of living in the now, although I have seen some adults with the same limited perspective. For the general population of teenagers in our culture, if they are thinking about what's for lunch at 10 a.m., they should be considered a visionary, because most kids don't think that far ahead. Joseph, even though he was young, always tried to look at the big picture. How do you look at the big picture? First of all, you stop and ask, "What is God's perspective on all this that I'm going through?" God's perspective is eternal, hopeful, and purposeful. When you think from His perspective, you find that it becomes much easier to handle the tough times.

When the going gets tough, what really matters is not what happens to us but what happens in us, because what happens in us will surely come out. And when it does, it reveals who we really are. Several people I know who have gone through tough times felt closest to God at those very times. I have known others who have gone through similar trials and who distanced themselves from God or became angry with Him. What was the difference? Attitude and perspective.

Of all the people in the Bible, Joseph had one of the best attitudes. His brothers sold him. His boss's wife framed him, and he was thrown into prison. Yet through it all he kept an attitude that was pleasing to God. He knew that God had a plan for and a perspective on his circumstances that would work out for his good if he stayed faithful to the Lord. He didn't know the whole plan, but God rewarded him for his faithfulness.

Respond
Are you going through a tough time now? If you are not experiencing some difficult circumstances right now, chances are a storm may be brewing in your future. Think ahead and resolve to say no to despair. God wants you to take on His attitude and gain His perspective.

Remember
When you learn to gain God's perspective, your attitude will change and you will be open to see the things He is doing through your circumstance.

Think Biblically

Read

"I seek you with all my heart; do not let me stray from your commands. I have hidden your word in my heart that I might not sin against you" (Psalm 119:10–11 NIV).

Reflect

In response to certain things, my dad used to say one word, and oftentimes it served as an entire conversation: *"Think!"* I remember standing on a pitcher's mound with runners on base and an 0–2 count on the batter. I would hear my father's voice from the dugout: *"Think!"* I remember running the mile in a track race. As I was coming around the second lap, I heard his voice from the stands, saying, *"Think!"* What did he mean in those contexts? He meant, "We have been here before. We have talked about this situation. Remember? We were in the backyard throwing catch when I told you that when you face a batter with an 0–2 count and runners in scoring position, never throw the batter a good pitch to hit. Remember? When you are running a race, figure out who the strongest runner is, hook onto that runner, and stay with him or her no matter what. Why do I want you to think? Because during the game with all the excitement, noise, and pressures around, you may not remember. So, *think!* You know what is right. You know what to do. *Do it.*"

In our culture today, individuals and groups tend to float freely between various worldviews or to adopt and modify pieces of different belief systems that guide their lives. The Christian

53

has a solid guide. It is the Word of God. His Word never changes, and it serves us well in this culture. By taking its wisdom to heart and applying its principles to our decisions, we are protected in an aggressive culture. We just need to *think!*

Respond

How do you control your thought life? Our world bombards us with thought-shaping messages minute by minute throughout the day. How are we to combat the onslaught of negative or seductive communication that can hurt us emotionally and spiritually? By filling our minds with the Word of God. Feed your mind with a steady intake of verses that remind you of His truth so that when times of temptation come, you will be prepared.

Remember

Your heavenly Father wants to speak to you through His Word.

Verbal Coaching

Read

"When Jesus saw his ministry drawing huge crowds, he climbed a hillside. Those who were apprenticed to him, the committed, climbed with him. Arriving at a quiet place, he sat down and taught his climbing companions" (Matthew 5:1–2 MSG).

Reflect

When I worked at a Christian university, I often had the opportunity to speak in the chapel. I loved it. Speaking to a diverse crowd challenged my communication skills. There were academics with PhD degrees and undergrads who had trouble spelling *PhD.* There were those who wanted to be there and those who could not wait to get out. Others came to do their homework, and still others zoned in and out of a seeming coma as I tried to capture their attention. I absolutely loved the challenge because I knew that if I could get their attention, then maybe God's Spirit could capture their hearts.

When Jesus climbed the hillside to speak to the huge crowd that had gathered, He faced a very diverse crowd. The crowd was made up of men and women from various cultures and backgrounds. It was a cross section of humanity. There were those who had experienced success in their field and some who were still trying to find their field. Some were failures looking for hope, whereas others were content yet curious. There were those who were well educated and those who were not. Obviously present were those representing various races and religious creeds. Jesus today is speaking to a melting pot of people who need direction, understanding, and hope. They are on the same quest together even though they do not know each other. They are all seeking. They need a coach.

Respond

I used to work with coaches. I found them to be driven people. As I see it, their expectations are always high and their discipline is relentless. Jesus coached these followers on the hillside with words of strong conviction and solid teaching. Many times He said, "You have heard it said, but I say...." In other words, He meant that there is another perspective to life than the one they were used to hearing. He may have said, "You have heard, but you have missed the point, so let me break it down for you. I will put it in terms you will understand." He always wants to make His message personal to you because that is how it can become powerful in you.

Remember

He can capture your attention, change your attitude, and coach you into a victorious life.

Win Over Worry

Read

"Look at the birds of the air; they do not sow or reap or store away in barns, and yet your heavenly Father feeds them" (Matthew 6:26a NIV).

Reflect

Worry can assault your attitude. The other day I spoke to a woman whom I would classify as a professional worrier. She loves to worry. She must. She does it with great frequency. In the few minutes I was listening to her, she told me she was worried about her kids, her job, her finances, her husband, her cat, and—believe it or not—the weather for the next couple of weeks. Note that most of these things are out of her control.

There was a significant reason Jesus did not want us to worry. Because it doesn't work! But not only that, it can consume your life and distract you from living a fulfilling life. Jesus said that birds do not spend any time worrying about where they are going to find their next meal. They do not plan ahead by preparing storage bins for their food. They do not plant seeds in the spring so they can have food in the fall. They do not fret over a drought or a flood taking away their supply of food. They simply depend on an unseen power to provide for them. As Christians, we realize that God is the One who provides for us. He controls the weather. He produces what we need and is always faithful to meet all our needs.

I have heard many people camouflage their worry by calling it concern, but it is still worry—and is still sinful. The answer is to put God's will and His righteousness first in your life. When you do that, you find that He takes care of the rest.

Respond

How much time do you spend worrying? Do you exercise faith in your heavenly Father and put Him first in your life? If not, you probably worry quite a bit. Beware, as worry can rob you of life, not only of the enjoyment of life but also of the number of days of your life (Matthew 6:27).

Spend some time right now turning your biggest worry over to God. Ask Him to help you focus on Him instead of on your problems. You will find He is big enough to handle all the things you are facing now.

Remember

Worry maximizes your problems and minimizes your God. So trust Him with everything.

Follow a Think Plan

Read
"And now, dear brothers and sisters, one final thing. Fix your thoughts on what is true, and honorable, and right, and pure, and lovely, and admirable. Think about things that are excellent and worthy of praise" (Philippians 4:8 NLT).

Reflect
One day the apostle Paul was sitting in jail and writing. He put on paper the verse we know as Philippians 4:8. In writing this letter to some friends in Philippi, he closed his thoughts to them by spotlighting where they were focusing their thoughts. The context they lived in was a world dominated by a ruthless Roman power that oppressed the weak and was dominated by a narcissistic philosophy. In the midst of that context, Paul instructed the Philippians to think in a different way than the world around them thought. Remember: he was in jail and facing death as he was writing this letter. He is an example of how to think differently than the world around you.

For most of us, our thoughts have patterns. We consider various things in our minds on a daily basis, and those things determine our attitude and outlook on people, situations, and life as a whole. Therefore, it is vital to know what your thought patterns are and where they are leading your life. How is it possible for you to think unlike the world around you, especially when that world is very powerful and aggressive?

Respond

To think positive in not so positive times, you need a "think plan." Paul suggests that eight things should dominate your think plan. Focusing on truth, honor, rightness, purity, love, admiration, excellence, and praiseworthiness, he sets the boundaries of a healthy thought life. But how do you get there?

First, you need to admit you need a plan and that your mind is a battlefield of thoughts. You can either control the battlefield or allow someone else to control it. Second, you need to surround yourself with people who think like you want to think. These are your attitude mentors. Third, be honest with yourself and recognize the things in your life that affect your thought life in a negative way. These may include situations or people. Avoid them, or at least minimize them. You can do this—and it will change your life for the better.

Remember

If you do not control how you think, something or someone else will.

For Better or for Worse

"In the land of Uz there lived a man whose name was Job. This man was blameless and upright; he feared God and shunned evil. ... His wife said to him, 'Are you still maintaining your integrity? Curse God and die'" (Job 1:1, 2:9 NIV)!

Reflect
I wonder if the phrase *for better or worse* was repeated at Job's wedding. If it was, it probably was repeated without a second thought, just as it often is today. We hear the words but never fathom what *worse* really means. Job's wife found out.

She probably had been attracted to her boyfriend Job because he was an honest, upstanding young man who said what he meant and meant what he said. However, integrity eventually got on her nerves when the crisis of their lives raised its ugly head and stripped them of everything. In a matter of minutes their lives were turned upside down, with no relief in sight. Yet in the midst of the storm, Job's attitude was one of trust in God regardless of the losses.

Job respected God and, as a habit of his life, kept himself away from sin. He was a faithful husband, a good father, a respected businessman, and the target of Satan's attack. When Satan attacked, it seemed to Job as though everything was gone, even the support of his wife. Perhaps she was so accustomed to the good life that she had forgotten who provided it. Maybe she was just stressed. Losing family and fortune can do that to you. Whatever the case, the circumstances left her bitter toward God.

But through all these crises, Job did not sin against God. He never played the victim card. As bad as Job wanted this chapter of his life to be over, God was the author and He wasn't ready to put His pen down. God saw Job through his crisis, maybe not in the way Job expected, but God did not abandon Job.

Respond

God is not finished with this chapter of your life. He is the one writing your book, and He's not finished with it. Whatever your situation, you can learn from Job. Stay faithful so you can live without regrets. Seek God daily, and you will find Him.

Remember

God knows your situation and wants you to look to Him.

Character

Character is who you are when no one is watching.

"People with integrity walk safely, but those who follow crooked paths will slip and fall" (Proverbs 10:9 NLT).

Courage: The Missing Ingredient

Read

"Be strong and very courageous. Be careful to obey all the law my servant Moses gave you; do not turn from it to the right or to the left, that you may be successful wherever you go" (Joshua 1:7 NIV).

Reflect

One of my favorite scenes in the movie *The Wizard of Oz* is the one where the Cowardly Lion stands outside the doors of the wizard's chamber and eloquently sings of the missing ingredient in his life. Several words are used to describe that ingredient: bravery, valor, audacity, heroism, confidence, guts, grit, backbone, spunk, etc. No matter what you call it, it's the missing ingredient in many lives today. What am I talking about? Courage. It is the character trait that is missing in many believers today. It makes the physically challenged reject pity and keep going. It's what helps every married couple dismiss conversations of divorce. It's what encourages the divorcée to face tomorrow. It's courage, and it's missing.

David had courage as a small boy. Elijah had it when the prophets of Baal outnumbered him. Moses had it when he stood against Pharaoh. Joshua had it when he led the children of Israel into the Promised Land. The fact is it is impossible to live victoriously for Christ without courage. In our effort to change our world for Christ, we are missing a key ingredient. We are educated enough and we have the right message, but we lack the courage to take a stand.

Respond
The truth is that we need more courageous people today in the home, at school, in the workplace, and in government. I believe a young person can be courageous in the face of peer pressure and not give into the temptations of the world system. I believe a parent can be courageous and tell his or her children no with steadfast determination when those children throw tantrums to get their way.

Courage is something you prepare to do. What will increase your courage level? God told Joshua to be careful to obey. This means that if you are willing to be obedient in your daily disciplines of prayer and Bible study, God will enable you to be courageous. It will take time and discipline, but it starts with you making up your mind to be courageous (read Daniel 1:8).

Remember
"I'm sure I could show my prowess. Be a lion, not a mouse. If I only had the nerve."
—The Cowardly Lion

Honoring the Family Name

Read

"And whatever you do, whether in word or deed, do it all in the name of the Lord Jesus, giving thanks to God the Father through him" (Colossians 3:17 NIV).

Reflect

Hufty. You say it—I've heard it. I am talking about the mispronunciation of my last name. Here are some classic examples: Hefley, Hufley, Huffy, Huft, Huff, Hufnee, Hefty, Hefty, Hefty. I get used to it and shrug it off, but it got old after a while. Why? Because my name means something to me. When I used to travel a lot and I found phone books in motels, I would get out the phone book and start scanning the white pages to see if I had a long-lost relative in that city. I never found one (Hufty is a unique name).

In the small town where I grew up, my family's name was respected, mainly because of my dad. His character was one of integrity, and he had a strong work ethic. The name Hufty was synonymous with respect. I remember many times when my dad dropped me off at a school event. The last thing he would say to me was, "Remember your last name." In other words, "Behave like you are a Hufty. Don't act like the kids who do not honor their family name. You be different."

I was taught to honor my family name. If I did anything that caused the community to look on my family with disgrace, I would greatly disappoint my parents. The same thing is true for the Christian. A lot is riding on that name. To be called a Christian is a great privilege, one that carries great responsibility. If I do or say anything that would cause believers and unbelievers alike to question my character or behavior, I am disrespecting and dishonoring the name of Christ.

Respond

The psalmist has written, "He refreshes my soul. He guides me along the right paths for his name's sake" (Psalm 23:3). God wants to guide us on the right paths of life, in the right decision-making plans, and in the right attitudes because His reputation is riding on our behavior. Are you honoring His name with your behavior?

Remember

If you carry the Christian name, make sure your behavior honors it.

Completely His

Read

"For the eyes of the Lord run to and fro throughout the earth that He may strongly support those whose heart is completely His" (2 Chronicles 16:9 NASB).

Reflect

Second Chronicles 16:9 is one of my favorite verses in the Old Testament. Notice that this verse does not read, "The eyes of the Lord run to and fro throughout the earth that He may strongly support those whose heart is divided or shared between Him and their selfish interests." No. You will never find such a verse in the Bible. God is interested in supporting those who are sold out to Him. This passage says that God is constantly looking for those "whose heart is completely His"!

What does it look like to be completely His? The phrase *completely His* in this text is the Old Testament equivalent to what the New Testament refers to as being "filled with the Spirit" (Ephesians 5:18). To be filled with the Spirit of God simply means to be controlled or guided by the Holy Spirit. But how do you know when His Spirit controls you? Does it mean you pray more than other people do? Does it mean you do spiritual things like go to church and read your Bible? Although those activities are admirable and helpful, they are not the true indicators of being controlled by His Spirit.

Think about Peter. You would think that after listening to and following Jesus for three years, he would be "completely

His." But after the authorities took Jesus, "Peter followed from a distance" (Luke 22:54), a sign of not being "completely His." Later, Peter tried to "blend in with the world" (Luke 22:55), another sign of not being "completely His." Finally, Peter "denied Jesus not once but three times" (Luke 22:56–60). These statements are indicators that in those moments Peter was not "completely His."

Respond

Notice the three actions of Peter highlighted in the paragraph above. Can you relate? Have you ever followed Him from a distance, that is, sought not to be identified with Him? Or have you tried to blend in with the crowd and not take a stand for Christ? Have you ever denied Christ? If so, at those moments you were not being completely His.

Remember

God is looking for people He can strongly support.

Counting on God

Read

"Give your servant success today by granting him favor in the presence of this man. I was cupbearer to the king" (Nehemiah 1:11 NIV).

Reflect

High-stakes conversations. Have you ever had one? Nehemiah had one with King Artaxerxes. He was going to ask for a leave of absence to rebuild the walls around Jerusalem. What chance would a slave have to make such a request?

After weeping, praying, fasting, and confessing, Nehemiah connected with God on a whole new level. He knew he could count on God. His heart had become so knit with God's heart that he developed a confidence to go before the king and make this monumental request. Only God knew the king's heart, so Nehemiah prayed, asking God to move in the heart of the king.

Nehemiah prayed that God would work in the life of the king to grant Nehemiah his request unusual, as it may have seemed. Once the king granted the request, the first challenge was completed. But just as life goes, so go the challenges of life. One challenge is conquered and another surfaces. After Nehemiah had gained the king's approval, opposition from those who did not want to see the wall rebuilt came in what seemed to be overwhelming numbers (Nehemiah 4:7–8). But Nehemiah was faithful and the wall was rebuilt. O that we would take a leave of absence from the world system to honor God with our lives!

Respond

What project has God set before you? What challenge has He placed on your heart? What wall is God asking you to rebuild—the wall of integrity? the wall of love? the wall of self-discipline? Do you know in your heart that you can count on God to accomplish what He has designed for you? Are you sad about the things that make God sorrowful? Have you prayed and confessed to Him the things that keep you from following close to Him? God wants to use you in a great way. Will you do whatever it takes to position yourself so as to be available for His movement in your life?

Take some time right now to praise and thank God for His dependability during the challenges of life. Your dependence on Him brings confidence and success to your endeavors.

Remember

Look around yourself. God may be positioning you for a great work.

Crowding God Out

Read

"Still others, like seed sown among thorns, hear the word; but the worries of this life, the deceitfulness of wealth and the desires for other things come in and choke the word, making it unfruitful" (Mark 4:18–19 NIV).

Reflect

Have you ever been on a treadmill? You are moving but not going anywhere. You are worn out with not a lot to show for it. This sounds like the routine of many in our society today. We are always moving and filling our lives with activity, yet we don't seem to gain a lot from the activity. Our lives get crowded. The sad thing is that we oftentimes, in our busyness, crowd God out. The crowded heart in Mark 4:18–19 represents people who are distracted by the cares of this world. These distractions draw people's minds in many different directions and leave little time for spiritual concerns.

The deceitfulness of wealth mentioned in this passage refers to the riches that present themselves as good, thereby enticing people to go after them. However, the promises that riches claim are deceiving. They are never realized.

All these things have a way of choking the Word in our lives. The result of this is that we are unfruitful as believers. When we are unfruitful, we make little difference in or impact on the culture. The reality is that the Word of God has many competitors that strive to influence us. Satan makes sure of that fact. These competitors strangle the effectiveness of the Word of God in our lives and produce in us a divided heart. On the one hand we want to be good Christians and serve God, but on the other hand we have allowed so many things to fill our lives that we end up compartmentalizing God in our life. We let Him have dominion over Sunday, but we put Him on the shelf the rest of the week.

Respond
Sometimes we find ourselves running so fast in trying to gather all the things the world has to offer that we end up running away from God instead of running to Him. Does that sound like you? Consider today being a wake-up call for you to reevaluate your load and your pace.

Remember
God can fill your life in a more satisfying way than can anything this world has to offer.

Doing What's Right

Read

"Moreover, from the twentieth year of King Artaxerxes, when I was appointed to be their governor in the land of Judah, until his thirty-second year—twelve years—neither I, nor my brothers ate the food allotted to the governor" (Nehemiah 5:14 NIV).

Reflect

Nehemiah was determined to be above reproach no matter what. He would not allow himself to do anything that would make anyone question his integrity. Before he made a decision, he would think through the ramifications of each option, considering how those decisions could affect his leadership and standing with the people. Even with temptation all around him and his stomach growling, he knew that his integrity would be more satisfying than the food allotted to the governor. There were probably well-meaning followers and admirers of Nehemiah who would tell him, by virtue of his position that he had earned the right to eat the food allotted to the governor. After all, he was the governor at the time. But Nehemiah must have known that endearing and flattering words from people during prosperous times can be shallow—and ultimately meaningless and forgotten when difficulties arise. Therefore, he decided not to take advantage of the privileges of his position.

Integrity is demonstrated both by what we do and what we don't do. Most of us would agree that knowledge is profitable and obedience is priceless, but all of us struggle with doing what we know to do. When the pressure mounts, we sometimes cave under the stress we carry. However, James said that for us to know what is the right thing to do and then not to do it is a sin (James 4:17). That means we will be blessed in our obedience regardless of the outside pressures we face. The truth is for most of us that we do not need any more knowledge or inspiration; we just simply need to do what we already know is right.

Respond
Spiritually speaking, what things do you know to do? Pray? Read your Bible daily? Give to God's work? Witness for Christ? Love the unlovely? Now here comes the toughest question: do you do the things you know are right? Jesus said, "If you know these things, you are blessed if you do them" (John 13:17).

Remember
Do what is right and be blessed today.

Eat, Drink, and Be … What?

Read

"And I'll say to myself, 'You have plenty of good things laid up for many years. Take life easy; eat, drink and be merry'" (Luke 12:19 NIV).

Reflect

The farmer mentioned in this story probably was a good man. Jesus never said he was dishonest. He never said he was a liar. In fact, by the world's standards this man would have been considered a great success. He worked long and hard for what he owned. So, what was the problem with this guy? The problem is seen in the first five words of the verse: "And I'll say to myself." In other words, the farmer was saying, "I will not consult God. I will not consider His perspective. I will not look around and notice the needs of others. I will only think about what I want and what I think I deserve." Look closely at the verse and notice the personal pronouns. He talked to himself as if he were immortal. He was on the throne of his own life, and to him no one was more important than he was. He would have fit right in with the me generation we are living amid today.

This man lived his life like many do today—by praising self and ignoring God There was no room in his life to acknowledge God. Perhaps this was because his life was already filled with all the good things he had laid up for many years. Did he ever stop to think of who provided all those good things? Did he actually think he was the only reason he was successful? We can become so focused on what we are doing that we miss *who* is really providing for us. Observe how God responded to such a greedy lifestyle: "You fool. Tonight you lose it all" (Luke 12:20). How final! How futile to live a life of greed!

Respond
One of the characteristics of the greedy person is that he shows signs of being so autonomous and so selfish that he ignores God. The truth is, life is not easy. Storing things up for yourself is good planning for a rainy day, but laziness is the Devil's workshop. Does that sound like you? Do you spend your time ignoring God or adoring Him?

Remember
Every good thing you have has come from God above.

Find Where God Is Working

Read

"No one can come to me unless the Father who sent me draws him" (John 6:44 NIV).

Reflect

We can be so egotistical sometimes that we think God exists to work with us on our projects. However, for me, some of the most exciting times in my life have come when I saw where God was working and was able to become a part of His work. So how does one know where God is working? One sure way to recognize where God is working is to identify what only He can do in a given situation. When you see that happen, you have a critical choice: do I become a participant in what God is doing, or do I remain a spectator? Spectators observe and assess a situation but never have a full experience. They go to the game and can observe what happens, but they can never feel what it is like to be on the field. The difference between those who join God in His work and those who observe God's work is a simple act of the will.

Today's Scripture shows us one such place God works. He works to draw people to Himself. Did you notice the word *draws* in today's verse? God does not drive people or force them. He *draws* them by His love. So, if you hear a neighbor or coworker asking questions of a spiritual nature, rest assured that God is not far away, *drawing* them to Himself. That is your signal to join God in His work.

Respond

Probably more times than not we miss God working because we simply are not looking for Him to work. We are so busy that we do not take time to see if it might be Him working in the situations around us. But God is always working. He works in boardrooms and restaurants. He works on playgrounds and in supermarkets. Sometimes He uses a kind act, and other times He uses a tragedy, but He is constantly working so people will somehow connect with Him. Have you noticed how God is working around you this week? What are you waiting for? Join Him!

Remember

God is interested in your joining Him in His work, not the other way around.

God Is Patient but Not Dismissive

Read

"We should not commit sexual immorality, as some of them did—and in one day twenty-three thousand of them died" (1 Corinthians 10:8 NIV).

Reflect

A history lesson is sometimes given in order to make a point. The apostle Paul, while writing to the Christians in Corinth, referred to the children of Israel back in Old Testament days who worshipped the false god Baal and committed immoral sexual acts with the Moabite prostitutes who worshipped Baal. God's judgment on them was swift and sure. Paul went on to tell the Corinthians, essentially, "Don't think what you are doing slips past the Almighty."

There are many areas where temptation can trap you. Sexual immorality is only one. But the traps are often the same in nature. They attract you subtly. No one gets up in the morning and says, "Well, let's see how I can ruin my life today." That's absurd! But the tragedy is that many don't prepare themselves every morning to resist the things that can ruin their lives. Instead, when temptation comes their way, they talk to themselves in ways like these: "No one will ever know if I ..."; "God is really not that concerned about such a little thing like ..."; "This is as far as I'll go"; and "I'll be safe." *Wrong!*

Respond

God's judgment is still real on those who make choices outside His will. He still hates sin, and He still disciplines His children who practice such things. I'm sure some of those Israelite men were pretty respectable in their circle of friends. In fact, some of them were leaders. But the secret life they led did not go unnoticed by Almighty God.

Do you think for one minute that your secret life will slip by God? Do you actually think that He will miss your behavior and thought patterns because of His busy schedule? You are sadly kidding yourself if you do. He is so concerned about your life that He even provides escapes from the snares that easily entangle your life. He wants to give you the fruit of a good, moral life. Pray today that God will strengthen you and help you take the escape routes He makes available.

Remember

God is patient with us but is not dismissive of our sin.

How Much Is Enough?

Read

"A greedy man brings trouble to his family" (Proverbs 15:27 NIV).

Reflect

Behavior arising from greed is ugly to watch. It is something people try to hide because it is unbecoming; however, it often reveals itself when there is something for the taking. I recently officiated a funeral where greed raised its ugly head and there was a clear division in the family. As much as I tried to calm the waters and promote peace, for at least during the time of the funeral service, the power of greed was prevalent before, during, and after the service. Ugly. One side of the family was so angry with the other that the former would not even drive in the processional with the latter to the cemetery. How sad.

In Joshua 7, we read about Achan, a man who lived and died in the shadow of the verse cited above. His greed cost him his life and the lives of his entire family. Achan's trouble began when he stole from the ruins of the fallen city of Jericho, which God had commanded him not to do. This greedy act resulted in the defeat of Joshua's army in their next battle. But much more than that, it resulted in great trouble falling upon Achan and his family.

Respond

Now you may say, "Well, we don't live in those days, when a person's whole family is punished for the wrongdoing of one." Yes, you are right, but that doesn't put to rest the timeless truth of this verse. When someone is greedy, someone suffers. Too often greed affects family members. Greed divides families and destroys reputations. Now think: has your family suffered as a result of your greed?

First, we must define the word *greed* as it is applied here. Greed is the desire for more, an excessive, unsatisfied drive to possess. When greed takes over your life, it blinds you to your priorities and strains your relationships. Therefore, it puts stress on the relationships of those closest to you. So, it's impossible for your family to escape the effects of your greediness.

Solomon, the writer of this proverb, should have known. He had possessions galore and family stress to boot. Hmm, I wonder if those could be related? Now that you are sensitive to what greed can do to your life, why don't you declare war on greed today. Start by giving something away to someone. Make it a surprise.

Remember
Greed sabotages good character.

Living Off Sound Bites

Read

"Do not merely listen to the word, and so deceive yourselves. Do what it says" (James 1:22 NIV).

Reflect

One of my friends is a gear head. He can fix anything mechanical. A few years ago I bought an old tractor, partly for nostalgia's sake and partly to get some work done around my property. The tractor was often breaking down; it was old. I asked my friend to come over and help me fix it (actually, he did all the fixing). Graciously, he came to my house and started looking at the motor. After he looked at it for a minute or two, I said, "The engine will turn over, but it just won't start. Do you think the points are sticking?"

He smiled and asked, "Where did you hear that?" Busted. He had me. I didn't even know what points were on an old tractor, but I remember as a child my dad saying that the points were sticking on his old tractor and that's why it wouldn't start. I had taken that little sound bite into adulthood and was now using it like I knew what I was talking about.

Oftentimes we live off our sound bites to try to get people to think we are more than what we are. We use language and terms to impress others, even though we might not completely understand what the sound bite means. Just because you can say it doesn't mean you understand it. True Christian character is manifested not in words but in action and demonstrations of faith and obedience.

Respond

When I was a kid, my dad referred to some people as "blowhards." These were folks who said a lot but demonstrated little. They could not back up their words with their behavior even though they wanted everyone to believe they were more important than they really were. In this Scripture, James implies that living off sound bites is not really living. Words become authentic when they are manifested in daily living. When God's Word becomes the dominant authority in your life, you allow it to dictate your behavioral and thought patterns. When people see that your behavior and habits match your words, it will be appealing to them and an indicator of authenticity in your character.

Remember

God wants you to live according to His Word.

Pleasing Him through Self-Control

Read

"For the grace of God has appeared that offers salvation to all people. It teaches us to say 'No' to ungodliness and worldly passions, and to live self-controlled, upright and godly lives in this present age" (Titus 2:11–12 NIV).

Reflect

In order to lead a productive life, you must do certain things. Just as important, you must avoid doing certain things. That takes self-control.

Daniel had self-control when he made up his mind as a teenager that he would not defile himself by eating the king's food (Daniel 1:8). Job had self-control when he chose not to curse God and die as his wife suggested he do (Job 2:9). Shadrach, Meshach, and Abednego exhibited self-control when they refused to bow down to the human-made idol (Daniel 3). All these men had impeccable character. They lived productive lives, mainly because they demonstrated the character trait of self-control.

The ability to deny oneself must be developed (Luke 9:23). It does not come naturally and it doesn't happen overnight. It is a day-in, day-out process that is tested by the circumstances that come your way. The more you develop self-control, the more God will trust you with His will.

Titus wrote that those who have experienced God's grace are being taught to "say no to ungodliness and worldly passions."

This does not mean we are not tempted. It does not mean that we are perfect. It simply means that when you have experienced God's grace, you will be so impressed and amazed by His love for you that you will not want to displease Him by chasing worldly passions. Is the reality of His grace in your life that powerful?

Respond

To have self-control means to hold oneself in. Proverbs 25:28 reads, "A person without self-control is like a city with broken-down walls." In the eyes of the Old Testament writers, a city with broken-down walls was a disgrace. It was a sign of weakness and vulnerability. You cannot let yourself get to that point. Make some decisions to get control of the out-of-control areas of your life. To have self-control, you need help—help from friends and help from God.

Remember

When you are fatigued and exhausted, you are vulnerable and open to attack. Ask God to help you develop self-control in all areas of your life.

Renewal Results in Action

Read

"So Samuel said to all the Israelites, 'If you are returning to the Lord with all your hearts, then rid yourselves of the foreign gods and the Ashtoreths and commit yourselves to the Lord and serve him only, and he will deliver you out of the hand of the Philistines'" (1 Samuel 7:3 NIV).

Reflect

Samuel called on the people of Israel to demonstrate their return to the Lord by getting rid of the foreign gods they were acknowledging. He must have thought if they were willing to get rid of the foreign gods, their actions would show the genuineness of their commitment to God. But ridding themselves of foreign gods was just the beginning of this spiritual renewal. Samuel also led the people in a time of fasting and of confessing their sins. While all this was taking place, the Philistines were positioning themselves to attack the repentant Israelites. In fear, the Israelites pleaded with Samuel to continue to pray to God on their behalf. The Lord blessed their repentance and Samuel's prayer by causing panic in the Philistine army. The Philistines became so confused that the Israelites were able to defeat them.

Respond

What have you done to show the genuineness of your commitment to God? What have you rid yourself of to show Him your unswerving commitment to developing godly character?

Godly character is more than a lot of talk. It is God's taking over your life to the point where you are eager to obey Him no matter what. Do you trust and love God enough to say to Him today, "No matter what you want me to do, I'll do it"? The question today is, do you trust God? Enemies may be positioning themselves right now with you in the crosshairs of their sights, but do you trust God? You may be praying like never before and it may seem as though God is silent, but do you trust God?

James tells us that faith without works is dead. Is your faith active? God is trustworthy and faithful to bless your active faith. He wants you to depend on Him so He can show you great and mighty things that you could never imagine. Let Him.

Remember
Authentic faith is demonstrated through action.

Rich in God's Eyes

"But God said to him, 'You fool! This very night your life will be demanded from you. Then who will get what you have prepared for yourself?' This is how it will be with anyone who stores up things for himself but is not rich toward God" (Luke 12:20–21 NIV).

Reflect
A man came up to Jesus one day and asked him to tell his brother to divide the inheritance of their father's estate with him. Jesus said, "Man, who appointed me a judge or an arbiter between you?" Jesus did not come to arbitrate our legal issues. He came to save us from the sin of this world. So in answer to the man, he told a story.

The story Jesus told was of a man who had gathered many treasures on earth. However, he ignored the value of storing up treasures in heaven. God called him a fool, not because he had a lot of things, but because he treasured the wrong things. Therefore, although he appeared rich, he actually lived in poverty. Let's learn this from this story: your true wealth is never determined by how you appear.

The man in this story had the corner market on appearances. He was not a crook. He was not a drunk. He was not a bad neighbor. He was not engaged in shady business practices. But realize that what you are not, never counts for anything. As we see here, you can refrain from being a lot of things and still be a fool.

The man in this story adopted the philosophy of many today. He determined to "eat, drink and be merry for tomorrow we die." God says that is what made him a fool. To live for this life alone is foolish.

Respond

Are you building any heavenly treasures? How do you do it? Simply make the things of heaven, such as love, joy, peace, and patience, your treasure. Love those things more than the things of the world and you will be wise.

Take time to praise and thank God for His goodness and for how He graciously meets your needs. Ask Him to forgive your greediness and help you put aside anything that takes the place of His heavenly treasures in your life.

Remember

Build up treasures in heaven, not on earth.

Run Away

Read

"No one is greater in this house than I am. My master has withheld nothing from me except you, because you are his wife. How then could I do such a wicked thing and sin against God" (Genesis 39:9 NIV)?

Reflect

Think for a minute about what it would be like to have it all. You have position, power, and prestige, and everyone knows your name. You are good-looking, you have money, and people listen to what you have to say because you have wisdom. You think you've got it all! But you actually don't. Then comes the rub: you are tempted with something you don't have. It can be yours for the taking, and you might be able to get away with it. Worse yet, if you don't go for it, you may be slandered and forced to lose everything you have gained. What will you do? This kind of dilemma faces men and women today more than we might imagine. The dilemma is the choice between what we know is right and what we think we can get away with without anyone finding out.

Joseph was a young man of faultless character. Notice what he did in the situation described in the above Scripture. He ran from the temptation. He could have stayed there and justified his involvement with the married woman. He could have rationalized it and said, "I won't do it again. Just this once should be okay." But he didn't. Even though his flesh might have been tempted, his heart had the strength to lead him to run. He knew that as tempting as it was, he would never outlive the regret in his heart for indulging in one night of passion.

Respond

Are you facing some strong temptations in your life today? Have you already given in to them? Have you justified them in your mind to minimize how bad they are? If that is the case, stop right now and pray for help. Ask God to give you the strength to say no to temptation when the opportunity arises. No matter how much the flesh wants you to yield, start running. Ask God to show you your weak spots. Pray He will protect you from the opportunity to sin. Ask Him to help you, when the opportunity arises, to become sickened by the thought of giving in.

Remember

One simple piece of advice when tempted: *run!*

And the Survey Says ...

Read

"But the fruit of the Spirit is love, joy, peace, forbearance, kindness, goodness, faithfulness, gentleness and self-control. Against such things there is no law" (Galatians 5:22–23 NIV).

Reflect

I have surveyed churches several times over the last ten years regarding the traits listed in Galatians 5:22–23. I have asked people to name the top four out of the nine traits mentioned that they need most in their life. Self-control is always at the top of the list. Everybody seems to know they need it. So what does the survey tell us? Probably that the most difficult thing for a person to control is him- or herself. Many of us today feel like our lives are out of control, and they just might be. Outside pressures and circumstances coupled with unmet expectations often lead to a discontented life that seems to be out of control. If this sounds like you, what should you do?

First of all, remind yourself that you can develop self-control in your life. God wants you to have it, and He has provided His Spirit to live in you so you can produce self-control. Now, do you believe that so far? If you have trouble with that concept, stop right here and read that sentence again until you accept it as truth.

Second, realize that to have self-control and say yes to it, you must also say no to some other things. That means, for example, that if you want to lose weight, self-control helps you say no to the things that will rob you of your goal.

Respond

God wants you to operate in the Spirit. So if you allow the Spirit of God to manage your life, He will help you develop self-controlling habits. What steps can you take to bring self-control into your life? Start with stopping some things, such as allowing others to control you. Many people who are out of control have yielded the control of their lives to someone else. They are people pleasers who cannot say no and end up being manipulated. Don't let that be you. Remember: in its simplest form self-control is a matter of saying yes to the right things and no to the wrong things.

Remember

God's Spirit living in you can help you establish self-control.

The Character Trait of Submission

Read

"Slaves, submit yourselves to your masters with all respect, not only to those who are good and considerate, but also to those who are harsh" (2 Peter 1:18 NIV).

Reflect

Insubordination. Passive-aggressive conversations. Victimization. Entitlement. These are all cancers of the workplace. The opposites of these cancers are submission, respect for authority, and loyalty. If you want to see if an organization will grow, look at the attitude and practices of the employees. If they are loyal, respectful of authority, and hard workers, the company will have a great opportunity to grow. But if the atmosphere is the opposite, the top performers will try to find another place to work. But what if the boss is the problem?

Peter puts his finger on the problem within the early church context when he mentions the necessity of submission. Submission is tough, especially when it's directed toward someone we don't like or respect. Nevertheless, we must accept this verse with all the others in the Bible. Obviously, Peter was referring to Christian slaves during the days of the early church, but the same principle applies for Christian employees today. We must be submissive to those who are over us, whether they are kind or unkind to us. If the boss is abusive or immoral, that is unacceptable in any context. But if the boss is simply difficult to get along with, that is not a good enough reason to be insubordinate.

Something should also be mentioned here regarding Christian employees taking advantage of their Christian employers. The rules of submission are still intact. Being employed by another believer does not give a person the right to be lazy or expect special privileges. God is still the One we are accountable to, and that should never be taken lightly.

Respond

Peter was absolutely correct in writing this verse because God made the rules of submission with our best interests in mind. Whenever there is insubordination, there are problems. This verse is God's attempt to protect us from these types of problems in the workplace. Remember: getting along with the boss is important, but getting along with God is much more important.

Remember

Loyalty and service will not go unnoticed by God. He will reward your faithfulness.

Substituting for God

Read

"When the soldiers returned to camp, the elders of Israel asked, 'Why did the Lord bring defeat on us today before the Philistines? Let us bring the ark of the Lord's covenant from Shiloh, so that he may go with us and save us from the hand of our enemies'" (1 Samuel 4:3 NIV).

Reflect

Options. Our world is full of them. Have you been down the cereal aisle in the grocery store lately? You could spend days just reading the boxes. Today, we all love to have options. The world not only gives us options in the grocery store but also gives us options for God. It offers us all kinds of substitutes for God in our lives.

The first substitute is ourselves. We want control of our lives. After all, who can call the shots for us better than we can, or so we think? "Nobody has the right to tell me what to do," we proclaim. But in reality, God wants us to know that He knows how to live this life. He created it and gave it to us. Therefore, since He knows how to protect us and provide for us, He desires that we take our cues from Him. But sadly, many of us deny Him the chance to guide us.

The second option is "stuff"—the stuff our friends have and we don't have. Possessions distract us from the God who gave us the stuff. The tragedy is that many times we don't have the stuff—the stuff has us. We serve the possession instead of the possession serving us. Do you wonder if that is how you operate? Try getting rid of some of those possessions. Is that out of the question? If it is, maybe your possessions possess you.

Respond

There are many more substitutes for God other than the two I've mentioned today. In place of God, you can put people, money, popularity, pleasure, and so forth. The Israelites made the ark of the covenant a substitute for God. The ark represented God's presence among His people, but it was not to replace Him. Notice they took *it* with them so *it* would save them. The question is, are you subbing anything or anyone for God in your life?

Remember

There is no substitute for God.

Take Control of Your Lack of Self-Control

Read

"When the woman saw that the tree was good for food, and that it was a delight to the eyes, and that the tree was desirable to make one wise, she took from its fruit and ate; and she gave also to her husband with her, and he ate" (Genesis 3:6 NASB).

Reflect

Self-control is a big part of character. How would you measure your ability to control yourself? Can you do without things that you are not allowed to have? They are within your reach and you can have them if you want them, but you were told you couldn't. How do you respond? Does it depend on who tells you no? What if that someone is God?

Have you ever wanted a car or some possession that you knew wasn't wise for you to have? Have you ever wanted something you didn't have the money for, but you just had to have it, so you used a credit card? Is that self-control? Not hardly. At one time or another, we all have been guilty of getting something we really shouldn't have gotten. So just own up to it. We all have lacked self-control at one time or another, so we need the Spirit of God to help us live under His control.

Respond

To overcome a lack of self-control, we first must admit that we need help. We must face the fact we are indulgent and selfish. We must take charge of our thoughts and dispel the desire to have what we can do without. Eve could have done without the fruit of the tree in the garden. In fact, her life would have been much better without it. Her lack of self-control literally changed the quality of her life. And the same is true for you and me. Our lives can be ruined when we fail to show self-control.

Thank God for His protection in your life. Ask Him to lead you today in a way that will glorify Him by your demonstrating self-control. Ask Him to help those around you who need to develop self-control. Ask God to give you wisdom as you serve Him today.

Remember

A person with a strong sense of self-control is well on the way to building a strong character.

The Cost of Selfishness

Read

"But Elisha said to him, 'Was not my spirit with you when the man got down from his chariot to meet you? Is this the time to take money, or to accept clothes? ... Naaman's leprosy will cling to you and to your descendants forever.' Then Gehazi went from Elisha's presence and he was leprous" (2 Kings 5:26–27 NIV).

Reflect

Gehazi was a man of great potential. He probably could have been the next great prophet of Israel, but he had an inner problem: selfishness. Selfishness robs many who have to have more. Gehazi had followed the great prophet Elisha; and just like Elisha, he had followed Elijah. He had great mentors. He probably was very gifted, a persuasive sort of guy. He was probably well liked. But when Naaman, a former leper, offered the new suits and treasures as a payment of appreciation for his healing from leprosy and Elisha refused, Gehazi couldn't believe it. He pursued Naaman, lied to get the treasures, acted deceitfully, hid the treasures, and rebelled against the one who trusted him.

Elisha knew Gehazi's character very well. "Was not my spirit with you when the man got down from his chariot?" In other words, "When you were sneaking around and allowing your selfishness to control you, didn't you know I didn't approve?"

Respond

Selfishness can make us do crazy, unwise things. Gehazi with all his potential, and all the opportunities God had given him, was blinded. He was blinded by his one desire: to possess things. What he didn't have had blinded him to all the things he did have. Does that sound like you? Are you allowing selfishness and the desire for more to blind you from all the blessings God has given you? If so, then stop. The payment for selfishness is too high. Ask Gehazi. As a result of Gehazi's lying and selfishness, he and his family became lepers. Leprosy was a daily painful reminder of his selfishness.

God had given Gehazi a close relationship with one of the greatest prophets. He saw God work through Elisha in amazing ways. Yet even though he had such a unique relationship with Elisha, he did not appreciate it. Can you see all the blessings God has given you? Are you appreciating all God has given you to the point that you are content?

Remember

God's desire for you is that you will be a giver, not a taker.

The Final Authority of Our Lives

Read
"Let everyone be subject to the governing authorities, for there is no authority except that which God has established. The authorities that exist have been established by God" (Romans 13:1 NIV).

Reflect
After getting a speeding ticket, I told a state trooper friend of mine that my cruise control must have malfunctioned. I remember that he smiled at me and said, "You actually believe that's the first time I've heard that, don't you, Tom?" Needless to say, he got a good laugh out of my excuse; nevertheless, he was not sympathetic. Why? Because on the highway, he is the authority. He enforces the law. He enforces what is acceptable and what is not. It's his job.

The job of people in positions of authority is to give cues as to what is acceptable and what is not. We have a choice as to what or who will be our authority in life. Many people today regard their own intellect—that is, their own ability to reason—as their authority. Unfortunately, the intellect is a faulty authority. God has established an authority for His followers, namely, His Word. His Word is the place we go to when we are looking for answers to life. His Word gives us perspective and principles that navigate us through the storms of life, if we will trust it and follow its instruction. His Word gives us direction on what is acceptable behavior and what is not. His Word even helps us to select acceptable associates and companions. By using His Word as our authority, we are protected from bad decisions that could be based on emotions or a lack of facts. His Word is the most reliable authority by which we can govern our lives. Yet many of us today make excuses for not following it.

Respond
What excuses do you use for not spending time in God's Word? Do you think your excuses are unique, or would God respond to your excuses by saying, "You actually think I haven't heard that one before?" Is God's Word your final authority in life? Do Bible principles dictate your character? God's Word will not change. It is trustworthy and dependable.

Remember
God's Word is to be the final authority of our lives.

The Joy of Living with a Purpose

Read

"Continue to work out your salvation with fear and trembling" (Philippians 2:4 NIV).

Reflect

It is no surprise to God that you are here. He did not wake up one morning and gasp when He saw you. He planned you, and He planned the purpose for your life before you were even a thought in your parents' minds. The tragedy is that many believers search for purpose all their lives without consulting or seeking Him.

So, what is God's purpose for you? It is for you to develop His character in your life in order for you to be a reflection of Him on earth all your life. Your job, first and foremost, is to be a follower and reflector of Christ. You accomplish that through the various opportunities He gives you daily. If you would look at your schedule each day and acknowledge to God that you want Him to help you fulfill His purpose for you through that schedule, you would be amazed by how that would affect your attitude and approach toward the day. The neat thing about your purpose is that it can be fulfilled in any setting. You can reflect Him no matter where you are.

Paul said that we must work out our salvation. That means that God has done a work in you, through Jesus, to produce love and righteousness. Now it is your responsibility to work that out in daily living. You are to produce the fruit of knowing Him. Potential means little if it is not accompanied by production.

We, as believers, have much potential. God has gifted us to do His work. But if we neglect that gift or refuse to do the work, our lives will be dormant and joyless.

Respond
What are you working out that people can see? When you know, understand, and then do your purpose, it brings joy to life. If you refuse to fulfill your purpose in life, life will be a frustrating ride. Take a moment or two right now to pray and ask God to reveal His purpose for your life. Take time to write it down in your own words and memorize it. As you go through your day, look at ways you can fulfill that purpose.

Remember
His purpose for you is better than any plan you have for yourself.

The Value of Prayer

Read

"Then Asa called to the Lord his God, and said, 'Lord, there is no one besides Thee to help in the battle between the powerful and those who have no strength; so help us, O Lord our God, for we trust in Thee, and in Thy name have come against this multitude'" (2 Chronicles 14:11 NASB).

Reflect

When my eight-year-old daughter, Mackenzie, lay on the ground in the backyard screaming in pain, I knew we had a crisis on our hands. She had fallen from the swing set and broken her arm at the elbow. I'll never forget Rhonda's prayer in the emergency room: "Lord, if she needs surgery, I pray You will select the doctor for us and he will make sure her arm is perfect again." The doctor came in, introduced himself, showed us the x-ray, and said, "It is a very difficult break; therefore, she definitely needs to have surgery, and it needs to be put back together perfectly." Coincidence? No, just the God of all creation giving comfort in a crisis through a few little words. You should see Mackenzie's arm today. It's perfect.

When Mackenzie saw her family gathered around her in that hospital room, praying for perfect healing, it just reinforced to her how we value prayer in all situations. Prayer is not simply something you do just before a meal or when a crisis hits. Prayer is a natural part of the Christian life.

Respond

When Asa prayed as he faced his crisis, he admitted that he was weak and in need of God. As we prayed over our daughter, we knew we were helpless to help her, but we trusted God to bring someone who could help her. If you're not facing a crisis today, be consistent in your prayer life so you will be in tune with God when a crisis comes. If you are facing a crisis today, whom are you trusting? Do not trust anyone but God and those you recognize He is using to minister to you.

We all face difficult times. Remember that God knows what we are facing and is available to help. Trust Him and please Him. Have faith in Him, and ask Him to work His will through your situation.

Remember

Prayer, the natural response of a dependent heart, is a discipline of godly character.

Those Who Have Time to Listen

Read

"And there were shepherds living out in the fields nearby, keeping watch over their flocks at night" (Luke 2:8 NIV).

Reflect

Have you ever been so project-minded that you didn't have time for people? Or, have you had deadlines to meet and would not answer the phone because you knew it would slow you down? If that sounds like you, may I suggest a career as a shepherd? Shepherding has its perks. The shepherds mentioned in the Scripture above were not that special. Nobody knew much about them. They were simple, common men laboring over livestock when their night was interrupted by a messenger who was so compelling that they had to go to Bethlehem and see the miracle for themselves. Joseph probably wondered why the shepherds walked into the stable. No doubt their arrival was a surprise to everyone there. In fact, the whole night was a surprise. But wait, that is how God chooses to work many times. He surprises us with His grace so we will focus on Him. He reveals Himself to the commoners—the ones who are not too busy to listen to Him. When we are not too busy with the agenda of our lives, we become candidates to personally experience His arrival.

King David of the Old Testament spent a lot of time in the pasture, taking care of his sheep and letting God develop his character before he became king. It was during those times that God revealed Himself to David. Right after the apostle Paul became a Christian, he spent three years in Arabia. During that time God spoke to him in a great way about his ministry. Throughout history God delights in revealing Himself to those who would take time to listen to Him.

Respond

How much time do you allow in your schedule to listen to God? Do you make it a priority each day to spend time with Him? What projects are on your agenda for this week? You are probably concerned that if you are interrupted, you will not be able to finish all you need to do. But try not to let your to-do list deter you from listening to God this week.

Remember

Interrupt your interruptions and listen to God.

Watch Out for Twisters

Read

"Dear friends, do not believe every spirit, but test the spirits to see whether they are from God, because many false prophets have gone out into the world. This is how you can recognize the Spirit of God: Every spirit that acknowledges that Jesus Christ has come in the flesh is from God" (1 John 4:1–2 NIV).

Reflect

For me, a game that is more fun to watch than play is Twister. If you look on the Twister box, you will see the slogan, "The game that ties you up in knots." I remember working with a large group of young people who played Twister with a twist to it. The twist? They put six Twister mats together and covered the mats with baby oil. As if that were not enough, they covered their hands and feet with baby oil as well. There were bodies everywhere. It was painfully hilarious. But as I watched, a parallel came to my mind.

Twister as a game can be fun, but there is nothing funny about people who twist God's Word to say what they want it to say. I have seen these twisters work before. They make their watered-down gospel believable and appealing. The problem is, years down the road those who believe the twisters of truth become the casualties of a lie.

There are those who twist the Word of God in such a way that it appeals to their fleshly desires. These twisters of the truth have been in the world ever since the Word has been in the world. Satan was the first. Remember what he said to Eve: "Did God really say, 'You must not eat from any tree in the garden'" (Genesis 3:1)? Whenever you run across someone who says, "Did God really say...?", you should watch out, as people like that are trying to twist His words.

Respond
The way to avoid being swayed by a twister of the truth is to be so familiar with God's Word that it will be obvious to you when you read or hear something that is not consistent with the Bible. This discipline will equip you for the "Did God really say...?" people.

Remember
"God's Word is given to us to teach us, rebuke us, correct us, and train us" (2 Timothy 3:16).

Where Can You Find Absolute Truth?

Read
"But as for you, continue in what you have learned and have become convinced of, because you know those from who you learned it, and how from infancy you have known the Holy Scriptures, which are able to make you wise for salvation through faith in Christ Jesus" (2 Timothy 3:14–15 NIV).

Reflect
We live in a world that emphasizes relative truth. In other words, truth is relative to the individual. If the individual believes it to be true for him or her, then it is honored as truth. Earlier, in the third chapter of 2 Timothy, Paul encouraged Timothy to stick to his godly priorities regardless of the times in which he lived. He told Timothy that the days in which he was living would be filled with difficulty. People would be deceived and deceiving. They would be depraved and capable of doing anything. (Sounds like Paul knew something about our day.) Seeing as young Timothy faced such a difficult period, where could he anchor his life? Paul's answer: in the truth of the Word of God.

Down throughout history, people have searched for truth. Pontius Pilate's infamous question to Jesus, "What is truth?", still rings out from the hearts of people today. In the verses above, Paul told Timothy that absolute truth is found in God's Word. As a Jewish boy, Timothy was taught the Old Testament Scriptures from about the age of five. During his formative years, his mother and grandmother were great influencers in his life.

115

Then later, the truth Timothy had learned as a young boy was positively reinforced by the apostle Paul.

Respond

Who have been the great influencers of God's truth in your life? Why not take a moment or two right now to praise and thank God for seeing your need for truth and for sending the right people in your life to point you to Him. Take some time to ask Him to forgive you for the times you have ignored His truth. Now, ask Him to touch the life of someone you know who needs to experience the truth of His love. Finally, ask Him to help you recognize the lies of the world and to give you the strength to say no to them and yes to His truth for your life.

Remember

Let the truth of His Word be your daily guide and develop your character.

Winning in the Face of Opposition

Read

"But when Sanballat the Horonite, Tobiah the Ammonite official and Geshem the Arab heard about it, they mocked and ridiculed us" (Nehemiah 2:19 NIV).

Reflect

"You're out of your mind." "You'll never be able to do it." "You don't really believe that you can make this happen!" Words of discouragement; they seem to follow those who are progressive. They followed Moses. They followed David. They followed Paul. They followed Jesus. So, if you have received a word from God and you have prayed and planned, expect to be opposed. But remember, you are in good company. Also, understand that those who mock usually have limited vision and are living advertisements for the status quo. But God moves in spite of them. So when you are tempted to believe them, don't. Focus on the vision God has given you. Then pray and plan all through the process of fulfilling His dream.

The Sanballats of today are those who say, "We kind of like things the way they are right now. Why should we change? God has taken care of us so far without making any changes, so why start now? Let's just maintain." What they fail to understand is that God never says that He wants things to stay the way they are. God is always improving, always working, always reaching, and always loving. His love changes things, and His vision is to bring every tribe, tongue, and nation before Him on the last day. This will not be accomplished by promoting the status quo. God is looking for people of valor, like Nehemiah, who can stay focused even when the naysayers are shouting insults.

Respond

One of the secrets to Nehemiah's success was his character. He had developed the character trait to focus when he was tempted to be distracted. Yes, he heard the opposition, but he kept working on the wall with a focus and determination that could not be dampened or swayed. If you have ever caught yourself thinking like a Sanballat, change your mind now, because you are in danger of losing God's hand on your life. Remember: He is looking for those who want to move with Him and accomplish His dreams. If the opposition sidetracks you, watch out, as you may be ignoring God.

Remember

I do not know of anyone who named their son Sanballat. But I know many who have named their sons Nehemiah. There is a reason for that.

Working for the Right Reasons

Read

"But when the young man heard this statement, he went away grieving; for he was one who owned much property" (Matthew 19:22 NASB).

Reflect

Why do you work? Is it in order to acquire money? Prestige? Power? Possessions? Why does God want you to work? I guarantee you that it is not for those reasons.

I wish I could have been at that spot in Judea during the time this verse was penned and know what I know now. I would have shouted at the young man. "Don't go away! It is not worth it! Do what He says and see what happens! Trust Him!" But the went away. The young man did not have to go away aggrieved. He could have gone away full of joy and fulfillment. But he left in grief because he knew he could not serve two masters. Tragically, he chose to serve the wrong master. This story assures us that even the greatest of possessions apart from Christ cannot give us lasting joy and pleasure.

Jesus knew that the man in this story loved material wealth. When he instructed him to go and sell what he had, Jesus forced the young man to determine his priorities in life. Even with all his good qualities, this young man still was lacking in His love for God. No doubt many considered him a godly person, but when he was asked to demonstrate his godliness by giving away his possessions, he failed the test. His problem was not that he owned a lot of possessions. His problem was that his possessions owned him.

It is assumed that the man in this story was one of the most respected men in the area. He was as good as any Christian today. But to be respectable in the eyes of people is not the same as being real in the eyes of God.

Respond

To be content with what God gives us is a mark of spiritual maturity. We all should have goals, and we all should desire to be all we can be in order to maximize our platform for Him, but we should all hold what He gives us loosely. For when we hold our possessions tightly, as did the rich young ruler, we run the risk of loving those things more than we love the One who blessed us with them.

Remember

Hold tight to God and your priorities will be correctly aligned.

You Have One Enemy

Read

"In your anger do not sin; do not let the sun go down while you are still angry, and do not give the devil a foothold" (Ephesians 4:26–27 NIV).

Reflect

You probably see it every day. It's on television. It's at work. Too often it's at home. It's anger—and it's destroying many lives. Have you ever had anyone say to you that he or she just has a bad temper and it is tough to control? The truth is, people can control their temper. Have you ever seen someone in the midst of having an argument when the telephone rang? Did you notice how the person changed his or her tone when answering the phone? Anger can be controlled.

Anger is an emotion that clouds our thinking and confuses our judgment. It can lead to danger in relationships rather quickly. Anger is an emotion that, when uncontrolled, can destroy relationships. It has torn families apart. It has injured relationships beyond repair. Uncontrollable anger is a character flaw that must be addressed before it destroys a person's life.

Notice what Paul said in today's verse about anger. If we don't control it, it will give Satan an open door to enter into our lives and begin the destruction process. If we do not want Satan messing in our life it is critical that we get a handle on our anger. Our problem with anger is that we don't focus it in the right direction.

As believers we have one Enemy. If you're married, your spouse is not the enemy. He or she, at times, may look like the enemy. He or she may sound like the enemy or may even act like the enemy from time to time. However, as believers, we do not fight against flesh and blood. Our Enemy is in the spirit world, and his name is Satan. When we focus our anger at Satan, we spare those we love and strengthen our relationship with the Lord and others.

Respond
Our emotional lives can be filled with clutter. In order to simplify our emotional lives, we must get a handle on our anger. If something is of flesh and blood, it is not your enemy. Get angry at the right things, that is, sin in your life, Satan, and his methods.

Remember
The next time you get angry, stop yourself and make sure you are angry with the right enemy.

Your Associates

Read

"Do not be misled: 'Bad company corrupts good character.' Come back to your senses as you ought, and stop sinning; for there are some who are ignorant of God" (1 Corinthians 15:33–34 NIV).

Reflect

The most important decision you will make in your life is what you do with Jesus Christ. In other words, who will be the master of your life? The second most important decision you make is choosing whom you marry or the person who will be your mate. The third most important decision you will make is whom you choose to be your mentors. Whom will you hang around and take your cues from on a regular basis? The reason for the third decision, of course, is that the people you spend your time with often influence your thinking. And if they influence your thinking, they can influence your behavior. For example, say you get married and you start hanging around people at work who do not believe in marriage. They may tell you that marriage is old-fashioned and temporary, that it doesn't make any sense anymore. Feeding your mind with those types of thoughts day in and day out is not healthy and can lead to an unhappy marriage.

However, the opposite is true also. If you have people around you who are authentic, who have integrity, and who do what they say, that will rub off on you. Now, I'm not leaving out the element of choice. Of course, you can be in a crowd of negative people and have it not rub off on you, as you have the power to choose. But if you are in the habit of being around negative people, watch out!

Respond
So, with whom do you spend most of your time, negative people or positive people? People who have godly values or people who have their own values? Age has nothing to do with this. Peer pressure has no age limits. Whom you choose to be around often determines who you become.

If you have given your life to Christ, Satan wants to influence you in a different direction. Beware of his tactics. Take inventory of those you spend the most time with on a daily basis. Take inventory of what you are reading and who you are becoming.

Remember
Those whom you allow to influence you shape your character. Choose wisely.

Faith

Without faith, you cannot please God.

"You can never please God without faith, without depending on him. Anyone who wants to come to God must believe that there is a God and that he rewards those who sincerely look for him" (Hebrews 11:6 TLB).

A Covenant to Seek the Lord

Read

"And they entered into the covenant to seek the Lord God of their father with all their heart and soul" (2 Chronicles 15:12 NASB).

"To pray is the greatest thing we can do. To do it well there must be calmness, time, and deliberation." (E. M. Bounds, *The Classic Collection of Prayer* [Bridge-Logos Publishers, Alachua, FL: 2001], 649).

Reflect

The first song I learned to play on the piano was "Heart and Soul." It was easy: four chords, three majors, and one minor. I never heard it sung, and I didn't know the words. All I knew was that it was easy to learn.

The idea of seeking the Lord with all your heart and soul is not so easy. It gets complicated when we consider all the distractions the world uses to sidetrack us from focusing on the Father. The phrase *with all their heart and soul* in today's passage can sometimes be overlooked. Today, we would say that means to be all in, or fully committed. The "heart and soul" of a person includes the mind, will, and emotions, all of which can be distracted, discouraged, and deceived by the Evil One. To be serious about communing with God means you consider undergoing a whole renovation of thought and desire. It means to be completely converted daily. This act of turning our will entirely over to the will of God is a daily task. To seek Him with all of one's heart and soul is to be part of the believer's daily routine. In essence, that is a relationship with Jesus Christ!

Respond

E. M. Bounds points out that if you want to have influence with God, you will not make prayer a hurried sort of exercise. It can't be hurried or casual; too much depends on it. That's why it is good for us to enter into a covenant with God, to seek Him above all treasures. For when we are converted and make Him our daily treasure, we can accomplish more than we could imagine—namely, becoming more like Him.

Remember

Seeking the Lord with all your heart and soul is only difficult if we allow the distractions, discouragement, and deception of this world to have a foothold in our lives.

A Most Important Evening

Read

"Are you not much more valuable than they" (Matthew 6:26b)?

Reflect

My wife, our son, and I were sitting in our family room watching TV when in walked my and my wife's daughter, Mackenzie. Her face was serious as she said, "Mom, Dad, I need to talk to you, just the three of us." For months and weeks preceding this night, she had told us she wanted to talk about becoming a Christian. She even called and left messages on our answering machine, saying, "Hi, Mom. Hi, Dad. It's Mackenzie. I need to talk to you about asking Jesus to come into my life. Have a great day! Bye." As a means of finding out whether she understood what she was asking, we answered her questions with Bible stories speaking of Jesus and by mentioning what He has done for each of us. Her inquiries became much more persistent and urgent until this night in December.

My wife and I walked into the living room, and Mackenzie sat us down. "I've been thinking about this for a long time," she said, "and I really want to become a Christian." We talked for a while. We read Scripture and talked some more. Finally, she asked, "Could I pray and ask Jesus into my heart?" We knelt down next to the couch in front of the Christmas tree and made the angels sing. Mackenzie's prayer without a doubt were the sweetest words Rhonda and I had heard spoken all year. It was a most important evening that we will never forget. Why? Because the most important decision our daughter will ever make was made that night.

Jesus said that even though God made everything, He made us special. In comparison to the birds of the air and all the rest of His creation, we are much more valuable. Why? Because He wants to have a personal relationship with us. The most important thing in life is having that relationship and developing it. Are you developing your relationship with Christ?

Respond
Take some time to spend with God today, praising and thanking Him that you are important to Him. Confess the times you have allowed the clutter of your life to distract you from what is important, that is, your relationship with Him. Finally, ask Him to help you focus on what is important today, because today could be an important day for eternity.

Remember
God wants a personal relationship with you.

Admit Your Need

Read
"For all have sinned and fall short of the glory of God" (Romans 3:23 NIV).

Reflect
I play golf, so I miss the mark a lot. I aim. I try. I make the effort. I miss. Unfortunately, that is what many people do today with their lives. They try to be good. But we will never be good enough for God because we all have sinned. That is why Jesus came to be our Savior.

Today's verse pictures someone aiming and shooting at a target but continually falling short of the target. That is what sin is. It is missing the mark of Christ. The "glory of God" basically means Jesus. We all have sinned and fallen short of Jesus. That's why we need Him. Sin separates us from God, but Jesus bridged the gap between God and us by dying on the cross and paying the price for our sin.

Some people are like the lost coin for which the woman in Luke 15 went searching. She searched her house relentlessly until she found it. And when she found it, she had a party to celebrate. Why are some people like that lost coin? They need a Savior from their sin, but they are unaware of their need. Like the coin, they are lost and don't even know it. They have been blinded by the world's system and believe they don't need God or the salvation He has provided.

One of the first steps to become a Christian is to be aware that you need to be saved from your sin. Until you are willing to admit you are a sinner and in need of a Savior, you will continue to be like the lost coin, separated from the one who loves you most—God.

Respond

You probably know people who are lost and don't know it. They may never read Romans 3:23. They may not ever attend church. They may never watch a Christian television program long enough to get the message. But they will watch you. They will tune into you and view how you live. By the behavior patterns of your life, they will have a chance to see Christ. By the way you live, they might come to the point of seeing their need for Him.

Remember

Only One can save from sin: Jesus.

An Hour

Read

"Then he returned to the disciples and found them asleep. He said to Peter, 'Couldn't you watch with me even one hour? Keep watch and pray, so that you will not give in to temptation. For the spirit is willing, but the body is weak'" (Matthew 26:40–41 NLT)!

Reflect

I remember the first time I led a group of teenage boys in an extended prayer time. Their typical prayers lasted only a few seconds or minutes. So this was going to be a stretch. The instructions were simply to spend time praising Him for who He is and to be transparent. I asked the boys simply to talk to God as if He were sitting in the room with us. After a time of praise and thanksgiving, I started finding it funny to hear things like, "God help me not hit Kelly, because she makes me so mad." This transparency got the boys on a roll. Before they knew it, they had prayed an hour. They thought they were so spiritual that they went and told all their friends, "Hey, we prayed for an hour! It was so cool!" Even though their humility needed some work, they were amazed that they could spend that much time with God and have it be meaningful.

Jesus prayed often and extensively. He prayed when choosing His disciples, He prayed by Himself, He prayed in the garden, and He prayed on the cross. When He approached the Father in prayer, He did so with a humble and submissive attitude. His expectation of His followers was the same. In the garden of

Gethsemane He asked Peter, James, and John to stay awake and pray. When He returned, He found that they had fallen asleep. His response was, "One hour? Couldn't you watch with Me even one hour?" That time frame seemed reasonable to Jesus, taking into consideration the challenges of the moment.

Respond

Jesus said for the disciples to keep watch and pray so that they would not give into temptation. There is a direct correlation between the lack of prayer and vulnerability to temptation. Jesus saw this in His disciples and warned them of their naïve approach to prayer. Prayer is a tool for battle. It's like putting on corrective lenses so you will recognize the Enemy when he approaches. It's also like an energy booster that strengthens you before you go into action.

Remember

Prayer is the language of heaven.

Are You Thinking Big Enough?

Read

"Now to him who is able to do far more abundantly beyond all that we ask or think, according to the power that works within us" (Ephesians 3:20 NASB).

Reflect

We sat in a choir room at the church on a Wednesday night. There were about thirty teenagers in the room. They were attending our Wednesday night Bible study after having gone through a rigorous day at school. There was no fanfare. This was just another Bible study, until we read Ephesians 3:20. After we read this verse, the question was posed, "What do you think God wants to do through us? If He is able to do *far more abundantly beyond all that we can ask or think*, what do you think He wants to do?" Silence. "Okay, let's take a week and pray about it. Come back next week and share what you think God is saying to you."

On the next Wednesday, all thirty kids came back. We read the verse again. "Okay, what thoughts has God brought to your mind that He wants you to do?" Some began to share. The thoughts began to take shape and become consistent. "Do you think we could host a youth conference at our church? We could get our kids to work it." Another chimed in, "I was thinking the same thing. Maybe we could get some speakers to come in and a band to do a show." Still another replied, "Yeah, I was thinking we could have some workshops that our leaders could teach and we could be hosts to guest leaders." The thoughts continued that night and for the next two years until these kids hosted a conference that ministered to hundreds of teens and leaders all over the Midwest.

Respond

Warning: Remember that what He is able to do is connected to the last part of the verse—"according to the power that works within us." How much of God's power is at work in you? Do you hate sin? Are you walking in purity with His power to overcome sinful habits in your life? Do you make it a habit to pray daily? Do you allow Him to control you? If so, ask Him to give you some thoughts that will enhance your service to Him.

Remember

You cannot even imagine all He wants to do in and through your life.

Believe

Read

"But God demonstrated His love for us in that while we were still sinners Christ died for us" (Romans 5:8 NIV).

Reflect

Believe is a verb that means, "to be convinced something is true based on some authority." For the sake of clarity, let's use this definition for the word *believe*. For example, when you go to a doctor to get a flu shot, you believe you received a flu shot by the authority of the doctor who administered it. He or she believes you got a flu shot by the authority of the pharmaceutical label on the bottle that says it's a flu vaccine. In order to verify the vaccine, the chemicals would need to be broken down and examined. This principle applies even to your name, which you believe to be your name by the authority of your parents who tell you it is your name. They believe you are their child by the authority of the nurse who pointed you out to them in the delivery room (are you getting nervous now?). We believe in very many things today because of some authority.

For the Christian, the Bible is the final authority. It reads, "While we were still sinners Christ died for us." It tells us that when we "confess with our mouth Jesus is Lord and believe in our heart that God raised Him from the dead we will be saved." When we believe these facts of what He did for us, we take a giant step in understanding what salvation is all about.

God's love for us is more than just a lot of talk. He *demonstrated* His love to us. Romans 5:8 implies that He did not merely send us a letter or a book that said He loves us. He expressed it by giving the greatest and most sacrificial gift possible—Himself. If this does not prove to us that God deeply loves us, nothing will.

Respond

Allow me to be blunt for a minute. If you have been calling all the shots for your life and it has kept you from giving your life to Christ, you are lost and you probably do not even know it. Why not start your new life today? Read Romans 10:13 and follow its instructions. I believe you can!

Remember

You can believe God. He believes in you.

Call on God

Read

"Then I said, 'Lord, the God of heaven, the great and awesome God, who keeps his covenant of love with those who love him and obey his commandments, let our ear be attentive and your eyes open to hear the prayer your servant is praying before you day and night for your servants, the people of Israel'" (Nehemiah 1:5–6a NIV).

Reflect

Nehemiah knew that if he was to meet this challenge of going back to Jerusalem and rebuilding the walls, it would take a lot of prayer. He persisted in praying day and night for God to work. Nehemiah knew that for this challenge to be met, God would have to do a work in the heart of a godless king. But when one prays for what God wants, there is no mountain too high for Him to move. God did move in the heart of the king, not only to let Nehemiah go but also to provide for his needs as he went. God has much in store for us if we will but yield to Him and ask.

Nehemiah spent extended periods alone with God. In the prayer above, we see him begin by expressing adoration to the God of heaven. He did not start his prayer by begging God to do something; he began by recognizing who God is: the God of heaven. And since He is the God of heaven, the God who made heaven and earth, He is qualified to work in the heart of the king, whom He also made. You see God can work on the hearts of people because He made them. Nehemiah, knowing this, called on God to work out the details of the challenge.

Respond

There is no limit to what a submitted heart in the hands of God can do. Nehemiah was totally committed to God's purpose to rebuild the walls. What are you totally committed to? Are you experiencing the power of God at work in your life? If not, then who needs to make the adjustment?

Take some time to praise and thank God for His continual love. Take the prayer of Nehemiah and put it in your own words. Pray about the challenge God is allowing you to face right now.

Remember

Call on God and great things will happen.

Camp Out; Don't Cop Out

Read

"Early in the morning Joshua and all the Israelites … went to the Jordan, where they camped before crossing over" (Joshua 3:1 NIV).

Reflect

I am not a camper. For me, roughing it is staying at a room in the Holiday Inn that has no king-size bed. The verse above takes place when the children of Israel were camped out before they went into the Promised Land. In fact, they camped three days before making a move. Why? It's likely they used this as a time of preparation. One thing for sure is that they were committed to go—but were they prepared to go?

When you are moving with God, you will not always have full disclosure before you move. Full knowledge requires no faith. The children of Israel were getting ready to make a move without fully knowing what they would face on the other side of the Jordan. And yet they acted on what they knew. They knew God had been faithful in their previous moves. They knew their leader was courageous. They knew they couldn't stay where they were and fully please God. Faith is not a step into the darkness; it is a step into the light. Faith is moving with God based on His trustworthiness. Faith is trusting God because He is trustworthy. Faith means you pray, trust, and obey. It doesn't always mean, "go for it." Sometimes it means "wait for it" or, better still, "wait for God."

Have you seen people act foolishly when they were going through a transition? They made no preparation, sought no counsel, made no definite plans, and in the end failed. After the failure, many of them became disillusioned and blamed God; others just disappeared in embarrassment. That was not God's plan. They had felt God nudge them in a direction, but they didn't wait for Him and prepare themselves to go when He said go.

Respond
Are you facing a move? Maybe yours is not a geographical move but is a move to raise your level of service to God. Wait for Him. In the meantime, prepare yourself. Get godly counsel and listen to it. The Bible tells us that God's people hear His voice and follow Him (John 10:27). Scripture also tells us that He will guide us in all truth (John 16:13).

Remember
If God is moving in your life, move with Him.

Confession to God

Read

"I confess the sins we Israelites, including myself and my father's house, have committed against you. We have acted very wickedly toward you. We have not obeyed the commands, decrees and laws you gave your servant Moses" (Nehemiah 1:6b–7 NIV).

Reflect

Confession can be a humbling experience. When we confess our sins, we open ourselves up to whatever response the offended chooses. Oftentimes that is the scary part of confession. We wonder how the other person will respond. Will he or she accept us? Will he or she become angry and turn away from us? Will he or she forgive? Will he or she be willing to restore the relationship? No wonder people have difficulty confessing and admitting they are wrong. It is a painful thing when you can't predict the response of the offended.

Confession need not be a fearful exercise when you are confessing your sin to God. He already knows your shortcomings. He wants you to confess because, until you do, the possibility for change will not occur. You must be able to agree with Him that your sin is hurting your relationship. Confession comes first, and then comes repentance.

When we confess, we call the sin what God calls it: *sin!* Then, through the reconciling work of His Son, our fellowship is restored. Confession shows how much we are in need of God. And finally, confession is a continual thing. When we think of our disobedience, it is important to confess it immediately. This restores our fellowship with God and keeps the slate clean so there is nothing between God and us. Nehemiah confessed the sins of His people, but he also included himself. He knew he needed a touch from God.

Respond
Nehemiah knew the relief that comes from confession. He knew that if God was to use Him in this great challenge of rebuilding the wall around Jerusalem, his sins had to be confessed. He could not work effectively with a guilty conscience. How are you doing lately in the area of confession? Are you keeping the slate clean between you and God? Do you make an effort to be completely clean? When you confess, you are in good company. Isaiah confessed (Isaiah 6). David confessed (Psalm 51). And you and I must confess if God is to use us in any significant way.

Remember
Confession is necessary for cleansing.

Don't Forget God

Read

"Each of you is to take up a stone on his shoulder according to the number of the tribes of Israelites, to serve as a sign among you, in the future, when your children ask you, 'What do these stones mean'" (Joshua 4:5 NIV)?

Reflect

Picture this. The Israelites are at the point of going into the land God has promised to them. But first they must cross the Jordan River. God instructs Joshua to have the priests carry the Ark of the Covenant into the river. When their feet touch the water, the river parts and the water stops flowing. The priests stand in the middle of the riverbed as the nation of Israel crosses the dry river floor. What a scene!

All Israel stood gazing as twelve selected men descended the west bank of the Jordan. They reverently walked out to where the ark was resting on the shoulders of the priests. They each pried a large stone from the bottom of the river, and then they marched back up to Gilgal, placing the stones in a huge unglamorous heap. This was not much of a monument, considering the great display of God's power they had just witnessed. But it was to commemorate God's delivering them from the Jordan. As the coming months would come and go, the Israelites would be engaged in battle. If any were to flee, these very stones would serve as a reminder to them that they were abandoning the God that had delivered them. If any Israelite would be discouraged and decide to retreat, when he saw the pile of stones he would remember where they came from, the bottom of the Jordan River. He would remember that God was real that day and would think that if He had delivered them on that day, He can deliver them today.

Respond
What reminders have you placed in your life to keep you from forgetting God and all He has done for you? Do you have any stones of remembrance that alert you to the fact that God has been real in your life? Take a moment or two right now to thank God for never forgetting you. Praise Him for His power to deliver you.

Remember
God wants you to set up reminders of His presence in your life so when you get discouraged you can remember He is real.

Expressing Your Love through Worship

Read

"O Lord, our Lord, how majestic is your name in all the earth" (Psalm 8:1 NIV)!

Reflect

The idea of worship is an interesting one. In our culture today, many think that getting together corporately to sing and listen to a minister speak is worship. Even though worship can take place as a result of that exercise, that is not worship in and of itself. Worship is not a service. But service is a result of worship. Many people come to a worship service to be challenged but not changed. When you have worshipped well, it is demonstrated by your service and obedience to God. Worship, in its simplest form, is focusing on God and doing what He tells you to do. Paul said that our reasonable act of worship is to offer ourselves to Him. That makes sense. When I have been given much and realize how much He has sacrificed for me, the natural response is to do something for Him that will please Him. Offering myself to God seems reasonable, since that is what He did for me.

As you grow in knowing God through the experiences of your life, a natural outflow of those experiences is a willingness and desire to worship Him—not just publicly but also privately. The goal of corporate worship is to get to know God better, giving honor and adoration to Him. This is expressed through many avenues: singing, calling on the name of the Lord, giving to the Lord, sharing His love, and studying His Word. The Bible records how people worshipped in public as well as in private. Jesus is recorded to have spent hours in private time alone with God, worshipping Him and seeking His will.

In today's verse, we see how the psalmist called on the name of the Lord. When we call someone's name, we are seeking that person's presence. When we worship, we seek the presence of God. We approach Him by giving praise for who He is and thanksgiving for what He does.

Respond
It seems that the times I fail to worship God are when I have just finished writing about worship, talking about it, or reading about it—when I have done everything except worship. So maybe now it's time to worship.

Remember
Offering yourself to God is the act of true worship (Romans 12:1–2).

Faith in Stormy Weather

Read

"His way is in the whirlwind and the storm, and clouds are the dust beneath His feet" (Nahum 1:3 NASB).

Reflect

Life is full of God-appointed storms. Sometimes we can see the clouds on the horizon, and other times they literally come out of nowhere to dump their load on us. But regardless of their pattern, we know who directs them. Everything that comes into our lives is either appointed by God or consciously allowed by Him. Nothing comes your way that first does not pass through His hands.

Nahum says that storms are the evidence of His presence. It is important for you to realize when the storm comes into your life, regardless of its intensity or scope; it is no surprise to God that you are going through it. Sometimes the storm is a result of sin and God is using the storm as a wake-up call for you to get back on track. Sometimes the storm has nothing to do with your sin but is the result of the sin of someone else—that is, you are suffering as a result of someone else's bad behavior. But regardless of the culprit, storms are still confusing and hurtful at times. They can cause destruction and havoc. But an encouraging aspect of storms is that they are temporary. They do not come to stay; they come to pass. After a storm passes, we can be better for experiencing it. As a result of your surviving a storm, God can use you to help others who will face the same challenges.

Maybe I should define these God-appointed storms better. They are those difficult, heart straining, emotionally draining events in our lives that remind us of God's control over our circumstances. We all face storms. Some may be relationship storms. We may be going through a financial storm or, maybe a storm of loss. Their purpose is sometimes to test us and at other times to correct us. But they always have as their goal to make us grow and depend more on God and less on ourselves.

Respond

Do you see a storm coming? Look closely. "His way is the whirlwind and the storm." *Note:* When you realize that God is trying to accomplish something through your storm it will give you a different perspective of the difficulty you are facing. Seek Him today for a greater understanding of what He is trying to accomplish through the storm you are facing.

Remember

Storms by their very nature are temporary.

Fitting into the Culture of Heaven

"If they had wanted to, they could have gone back to the good things of this world. But they didn't want to. They were living for heaven. And now God is not ashamed to be called their God, for he has made a heavenly city for them" (Hebrews 11:15-16 TLB).

Reflect

I have had the opportunity over the years to hire several people for various positions. I have a template, one that did not originate with me, which I follow. I ask several questions, but all the questions are designed to determine if the candidate meets three major requirements. The first big requirement is that the person has the ability to do the job. I want to know if the candidate's skills give him or her the capacity to do the job and to improve what we at the organization are already doing. This helps me know if the person is competent. The second requirement I seek to discover is if the person would enjoy doing the job, not merely have a job that pays. Determining this helps me measure the person's motivation. The third requirement is determined by asking many different questions, but the gist is this: can we in the organization put up with the candidate, and can the candidate put up with us? This is a chemistry question. I am asking if the person can fit into our organizational culture.

Spiritually, God is not hiring us for a job. He is compelling us to join Him as He works. But the interview questions are not much different. He wants to develop our skills for His kingdom's sake. He wants us to experience joy in the process. And finally, He wants us to know that He can work with us, simultaneously letting us know that in order to fit into His kingdom we must be willing to work with Him.

Respond

If you are a believer, He is your boss. He allows you to be a part of His family not based on your competence but on your receptivity to His love. By receiving His forgiveness He equips you to serve Him on earth and fits you for your eternal place in heaven that He is preparing for you.

Remember

Right now, God is preparing you for heaven.

Giants

Read

"As soon as the Israelite army saw him, they began to run away in fright. ... 'Don't worry about this Philistine,' David told Saul. 'I'll go fight him'" (1 Samuel 17:24, 32 NLT)!

Reflect

I never felt at home in a weight room. Two things led me to feel intimidated: (1) weights and (2) guys who could lift them. I went out for football during my freshman year in high school, tipping the scales at about 110 pounds. My string-like arms and chicken legs were no match for the football players who roamed the weight room. They knew how to use all the machines and were well aware of their capabilities. For me the weight room was not the place to make an impression. I learned something during that time: I loved football but not the training it took to be a good football player.

Giants come in all shapes and sizes. Some are financial, others are emotional, and some are mental, but they are all intimidating. Giants bark out at your inadequacies and shout at your limitations. They challenge your faith and question your commitment. These giants are like heavy lifters in the weight room of life. They can be intimidating to people with smaller frames by simply making an appearance. Their outer shell threatens you and oftentimes leaves you paralyzed in fear.

David was a young man who didn't see a giant as something to run from but as something to refute. When he heard Goliath hurling insults toward his God, he quickly went into action. Why wasn't David intimidated? Because he had trained well. He had spent years dealing with giants of another kind. While David was a shepherd, he had to fend off predators that were attempting to harm his sheep. He had trained before he met Goliath, and all his training paid off. He dropped Goliath like a bag of dirt and put the enemy on the run. How? It wasn't because the giant was huge; it was because the training God had taken David through before he met the giant was sufficient.

Respond
How well do you train to be victorious over your giants? God never promised there would not be giants. He simply said He would take responsibility for them. If we submit to His training, He will prepare us for victory.

Remember
Training reduces intimidation.

Are You Okay?

Read

"And he said: 'Truly I tell you, unless you change and become like little children, you will never enter the kingdom of heaven'" (Matthew 18:3 NIV).

Reflect

One day I was playing golf with a friend and we started talking about his relationship with God. I asked him, "How are you doing spiritually?" He said, "God and I are okay." I said, "Tell me what that means and what that looks like when you say, 'God and I are okay.'" He said, "Well, you know, I do my thing and God does His. We are okay." Realizing he didn't want to go any further with this topic, I took the risk of digging a little deeper (I was really losing the round of golf—bad). I said, "So I think I know why you said you're okay. You probably have money in the bank and no big critical things happening in your life, but how do you know He is okay? Did He tell you He's okay?" My friend laughed nervously and said, "Well, He doesn't talk much to me. He's pretty busy."

His view of God was that God is distant and not interested in his personal life. He thought that God was someone to call on during a crisis, but as long as there was no crisis, he should let God do His thing and would call on Him when he needed Him. If you hold God at a distance in your life, you dilute His power. But if you hold Him close and personal, He will become a powerful force in your life.

Respond

Do you view God as distant? Do you view Him as angry all the time at what you have done? If so, you have a misconception of what He is really like. He is a life-changing God. He can change a hateful man into a loving man. He can change a prejudiced person and make her all-inclusive. He can change a bitter person to one who is filled with peace. He is the God of grace. He, knowing what we deserve as sinners, took the punishment we deserved so we can experience life. God is not distant. He is close enough to change your life if you will let Him. Are you really okay?

Remember

God wants to have a personal relationship with you.

Hearing God Speak

"He who belongs to God hears what God says. The reason you do not hear is that you do not belong to God" (John 8:47 NIV).

Reflect
When our children were small and my wife and I put them to bed at night, we would ask them before we prayed, "What was your favorite part of the day?" They would answer something like, "Riding my bike" or "Playing with a friend," to which we would respond, "Okay, let's pray and thank God for that friend [or for the bike] God gave you." We would try to show our children how to praise and thank God and to give God credit for everything He had given them. In so doing, we taught them how to speak to God. But how do we learn to listen to God?

Here are some tips on hearing God speak. First, you must understand that He speaks in different ways. To Elijah, it was in a still, small voice. To Moses, it was through a burning bush. To Gideon, it was from a damp fleece and then from a dry one. God speaks in ways that will get your individual attention. Not everyone has a burning bush experience, but as you read His Word you can understand this—He wants to speak to you.

Second, when God speaks, He speaks clearly. God is a good communicator. Throughout history, He has guided those who would seek and listen to Him. Paul said, "For God is not the author of confusion, but of peace, as in all churches of the saints" (1 Corinthians 14:33 KJV).

Finally, in Scripture, when God spoke to people, He didn't always reveal the whole picture. God told Abraham that he would father a nation, but He didn't tell him all that he would have to go through or even if he would see it take place. God told Moses he would lead His people out of slavery, but how Moses was to accomplish that mission was revealed step by step.

Respond
God is a revealing God. He wants to speak to you today. Will you listen? In order to hear Him, perhaps you must get away from the noise of this world. Get alone and be with Him and His Word. Offer yourself to Him. Then ask Him to speak to you.

Remember
God is constantly speaking. Are you listening?

His Ocean of Love

"For God so loved the world that he gave his one and only Son, that whoever believes in Him shall not perish but have eternal life" (John 3:16 NIV).

Reflect
Have you ever had a chance to sit on a beach and watch the activities around you? Several years ago, I wrote these words in my journal as I sat on a beach in Florida:

> The sights and sounds I am experiencing right now include crashing waves, endless water, and children playing. Children playing? How ironic in one setting to see the Atlantic Ocean, one of God's most massive creations, and children, one of His most fragile creations, side by side.

That reminds me of the story of the woman who felt a little seasick as she stood on the edge of the ship. One of the officers came up to her and asked, "Ma'am, are you okay?" She replied as she looked at all the water, "It's so big!" The officer then said, "Yes, and that's just the top of it."

God's love is just like that ocean. It reaches to depths that we will never fully know, yet it is shallow enough for children to enjoy. It is more magnificent than our finite minds can comprehend, yet it is for us—specifically.

Respond

How deep have you gone into the ocean of God's love? Have you been able to tread in the depths of His love to the point that your devotion to Him is unmatched by any other thing in your life? Do you enjoy swimming in the depths of His love, or would you rather play near the shore and wade in the elementary level of the Christian life? The point of the ocean metaphor is to communicate that His love for you is endless. You cannot exhaust its depths or fathom its capacity. His love is beyond what your mind can comprehend. "However, as it is written: 'What no eye has seen, what no ear has heard, and what no human mind has conceived'—the things God has prepared for those who love him" (1 Corinthians 2:9 NIV). His love is like nothing we have ever experienced. It is unconditional, unwavering, undaunted, unalterable, unexplainable, unquestionable, unexpected, and unbelievable.

Remember

His love is deeper and greater than any love you will ever experience on earth.

Hope in Disguise

Read

"But he was pierced for our transgressions, he was crushed for our iniquities" (Isaiah 53:5 NIV).

Reflect

On Palm Sunday in 1865, our nation was changed at a place called Appomattox. It was there that the terms of the Confederate Army's surrender were discussed. As General Ulysses S. Grant entered the courthouse, you would not have picked him out as a great conqueror. His boots were mud-splattered, he was wearing a private's coat, and only the epaulets on his shoulders indicated his rank. Quite a contrast was General Lee. Dressed in his spotless uniform, he looked the part of a great leader. Anyone looking upon this scene would have thought Lee was the victor. But looks are deceiving.

When Jesus came on the scene, He did not look like a conqueror either. In fact, centuries before, the prophet Isaiah said that He would not look like a conqueror. Hope has come into the world through the disguised package of a man, but not just any man—this Man is the Son of God. How fickle the world was then and is now. We put too much trust in appearances. Yet God's incredible work of redemption was accomplished through the unimaginable work of God becoming a man.

Respond

From the beginning God has not been impressed by the outward appearance of human beings. He told the prophet Samuel, "Man looks at the outward appearance, but the Lord looks at the heart" (1 Samuel 16:7). No one doubted who the conqueror was when the leaders walked out of that courthouse in Appomattox, Virginia, on April 9, 1865. The same is true for those who know that the tomb is empty today. The Scriptures plainly teach that Jesus has conquered Satan—and the penalty for sin—by His death and subsequent resurrection from the dead.

The prophet Isaiah foretold this victory over sin hundreds of years before it happened. He drew the picture just as it took place centuries later when he said, "He was pierced for our transgressions, he was crushed for our iniquities, the punishment that brought us peace was on him, and by his wounds we are healed." God's required penalty for sin (death of the innocent) was paid. As a result we are set free.

Remember

God's sacrificial salvation plan was for you.

How Can You Know That You Know?

Read

"I write these things to you who believe in the name of the Son of God so that you may know that you have eternal life" (1 John 5:13 NIV).

Reflect

Today's Scripture is one of my favorites in the Bible because of the word *know*. I've talked to many people who had no clue as to where they stood with Christ. I've asked, "If you were to die in an accident, do you know where you would spend eternity?" Many times the answer has been, "No" or "I think I'd go to heaven" or "I hope I'll go to heaven." Today's verse tells us that we can know where we will spend eternity. It does not say that we have to die on a "good" day or that we will have to guess about our eternity; it says we can *know* for sure. So, how can you know?

First of all, the beginning of this verse indicates that you may know you have eternal life if you are one who believes in the name of the Son of God. This is essential, but you must remember that this does not entail merely saying you believe. It means allowing that belief to direct your life. Remember that the Bible says the demons also believe, and shudder (James 2:19). So what other things may help you know you are a Christian? Jesus said, "He who endures unto the end, shall be saved" (Matthew 24:13). Therefore, endurance and staying true to your faith in Christ is another indication that helps you know you are saved. Still another attribute of a true believer is a hatred of sin. After you have been truly saved, you never look at sin the same way.

Respond
God loves you so much that He does not want you to be uncertain about where you stand with Him. He has gone to great lengths to provide your salvation, so He wants you to know, without a doubt, that you are forever in His family. Have you told Him that you believe in Him and His resurrection? Have you called on Him to save you (Romans 10:13)? Have you asked Him to forgive you of all your sins (1 John 1:9)? If you have and you meant it, you have been born again.

Remember
You must be born again.

It's a Head and Heart Thing

Read

"If you declare with your mouth, 'Jesus is Lord,' and believe in your heart that God raised him from the dead, you will be saved. For it is with your heart that you believe and are justified, and it is with your mouth that you profess your faith and are saved" (Romans 10:9–10 NIV).

Reflect

Have you ever been to a sporting event like a basketball or football game and watched a team get destroyed because of their attitude? They knew all the plays. They had the game plan in their minds, but they didn't have the heart to pull it off. I saw a game like that just the other day. There is no way this team should have lost. On paper they were much better than their opposition. But they had no heart and held bad attitudes.

It can happen in the game of life as well as in the spiritual realm. People have the head-based knowledge about what Jesus did on the cross for them. They come to every game (go to church), but somehow they miss the heart thing—the change that takes place when God takes over.

In Jesus' day, there were many religious leaders who made it extremely difficult and complicated to have a relationship with God. When Jesus came on the scene, one of His objectives was to simplify the process. He didn't focus on all the negative commands the Pharisees used as a litmus test to determine an authentic relationship with God. He focused on the positive act of developing a personal relationship with God the Father through a personal faith in the Son.

Respond
God has made it really easy for us to have a relationship with Him. He has done all the work. Our job is simply to confess with our mouth that Jesus is Lord and believe in our heart that God raised Him from the dead. We simply accept the work He has already done for us on the cross. Aren't you glad God did not make it so we had to look a certain way to get into heaven? Aren't you glad He didn't make it so we had to do a certain number of good deeds in order to be accepted by Him? Just believe and give your life to Him.

Remember
He wants to transform your life. It starts in the mind and moves to the heart.

Keep Remembering

Read
"Be careful that you do not forget the Lord, who brought you out of Egypt, out of the land of slavery" (Deuteronomy 6:12 NIV).

Reflect
I'm sure this has happened to you. You see someone at a restaurant or social event. The person recognizes you, but you don't recognize him. Oh, you may have seen the face, but you can't think of the name to save your life. Then the individual strikes up a conversation with you. What do you do? What have you done? Did you fake it? Did you play along? Or were you honest enough to say, "Please forgive me, but I've forgotten your name." I shamefully admit I've played along only to be embarrassed later.

It is said that the memory is the first thing to go, but that doesn't wash with God. He expects us to remember Him and to take measures to do so. In fact, He has given us exercises that are designed to help us remember how good He is to us. For example, participating in the Lord's Supper is an exercise in remembrance. Tithing and giving of our financial resources reminds us that all we have belongs to God. Some holidays are designed to pull us away from the world and to remember Him. Gathering together each week with believers is a method of remembering God and His faithfulness to us.

The nation of Israel was warned that when they came into prosperity, they should be careful not to forget God. Prosperity has a way of distracting us away from the One who allowed us to become prosperous. If we can properly handle success, we can handle most anything, because success has an intoxicating element to it that causes us to become numb to God.

Respond

The nation of Israel never intended to become numb toward God. But then none of us ever plans to forget Him. So why do we forget Him? We get busy, and slowly become lulled to sleep by the world system. When we wake up, we find ourselves bound by things that shouldn't even be a part of our lives. Then when we try to get out of the sinful traps, the natural consequences of those traps cause us so much pain that we often give up and settle for lower standards of commitment to Him. What happened? How did this happen? We forgot Him.

Remember

Don't forget God. He remembers you every day.

Knowing God through Experience

Read

"God said to Moses, 'I AM WHO I AM. This is what you are to say to the Israelites: "I AM has sent me to you"'" (Exodus 3:14 NIV).

Reflect

For years I have studied the Scripture. I intellectually know many of the names given to God in the Bible. For example, He is my refuge and strength, my Defender, my Deliverer, my Comforter in sorrow, the Bread of Life, my Counselor, my Savior, and the King of Kings. But until I experienced Him as *my* deliverer, refuge, and strength, those names were only names I read on a page in the Bible. I did not understand the true meaning of what it was like to have God be the being described by those names in my life until He met those needs in my life.

When I messed up and knew what I deserved, He was my righteous judge. My respect for Him was ignited and I was without excuse in His presence. When I repented, I experienced Him as my Savior, deliverer, and refuge. I sensed His mercy and He restored my peace. When I felt alone, He became my Comforter. It's just as he told Moses: "I am everything you need." And not only is He what I need, but also He provides what I need as I seek Him. It was through these experiences in my life that God revealed Himself and I discovered more of who He is and how He wants to be more in my life.

Too many people today shut God out of the experiences they go through. They wait for a crisis to hit before they turn to Him.

But if they really want to experience God, they need to look for Him in every experience of life. He's there, wanting to become real to them in their experiences.

Respond
If you need wisdom, He is the great Counselor. If you need peace, He is the Prince of Peace. If you need protection, He is the shield. If you need friends, He is a friend that stays closer than a brother. If you need grace, go to His throne that takes on the same name. He is everything you need. Paul wrote, "My God will meet all your needs according to the riches of his glory in Christ Jesus" (Philippians 4:19 NIV). Jesus is ready, willing, and able to take care of you and all your needs.

Remember
He is all you need.

Listening for Crickets

Read

"Then Joshua fell facedown to the ground in reverence, and asked him, 'What message does my Lord have for his servant'" (Joshua 5:14 NIV)?

Reflect

Years ago I heard a story told of a man from India who was walking in New York City with a friend when, in the middle of Manhattan, the man from India grabbed his friend's arm and whispered, "I hear a cricket." "Impossible!" his friend said over the sound of blaring horns and the roaring subway. But the visitor from India led his friend down the street to a large cement planter where a tree was growing. He then dug into the mulch and lifted out a cricket. What we hear is often determined by what our mind is thinking at the time.

Are you a good listener? I know some great people who have accomplished some amazing things but who are really not good listeners. Why do you think people are not good listeners? Perhaps it is because they have their own agenda. Perhaps it is because they lack focus. Regardless, not listening is a cousin to not respecting. Notice Joshua's response in today's verse. Joshua first showed respect, falling "facedown to the ground in reverence," and that prepared him to listen.

Before Joshua went into battle, he spent time communicating with the Lord. In fact, he was in constant communication with the Lord. He was so in tune with the direction God was giving him that anything to the contrary would have been obvious to him.

Respond
We need to be in tune with what God is saying. We need to develop the practice of listening for the voice of God, letting the beauty of His Word fill our minds even when the sounds of the world are crying out for our attention.

How do you get in tune with God? God doesn't use the same methods with everyone. However, He knows what it takes to get your attention. Perhaps it is a restless spirit, a word from another godly person, a blessing, or unusual circumstances. Whatever God uses to get your attention, nothing takes the place of His Word. He will confirm His direction through His Word. That is why it is essential that you measure every voice you hear with God's Word.

Remember
God wants you to listen to Him.

Living without Worry

Read

"Therefore I tell you, do not worry about your life, what you will eat or drink; or about your body, what you will wear. Is not life more important than food, and the body more important than clothes" (Matthew 6:25 NIV)?

Reflect

A hundred years from now, who will care if you wore designer jeans? A hundred years from now, will it matter what your social status was? As a believer, you need to think more from an eternal perspective. According to Jesus, the meaning of life cannot be found in physical things. Life is much more than what you see. Jesus used the physical things of life to illustrate His place in our life—He is the provider and Sustainer of life. Therefore, you have nothing to worry about, for it is He who cares for your physical needs.

God does not want worry to take up any place in the lives of believers. Why? Because when we are worrying, we are not trusting Him. God wants us to trust Him to handle the things we worry about. We can spend too much of our lives reading and reporting bad news instead of living good news. To end worry in our lives, we must put an end to the habits that lead us to worry. For example, I never say to my wife, "I really need a shot of encouragement today; I think I will watch the TV news."

Years ago, Frank Minirth and Paul Meier wrote that probably 98 percent of the things you are anxious about never happen

(Frank Minirth and Paul Meier, *Happiness Is a Choice* [Grand Rapids: Baker, 1978], 171). No wonder Jesus was so emphatic about the believer's not worrying! Worrying just isn't worth it. It causes anxiety and, sometimes, physical illness.

Respond
Your goal is to grow spiritually, which will never happen if you always worry. God knows your circumstances. They are no surprise to Him, and He knows what you need in the midst of those circumstances. So, to worry that your needs will not be taken care of is simply to waste precious time that you could use to concentrate on Jesus and the progress of your spiritual growth. Jesus, not your worries, should be the focus of your mind.

Remember
Worry is a waste of time.

Loss

Read

"Can anything ever separate us from Christ's love? Does it mean he no longer loves us if we have trouble or calamity, or are persecuted, or hungry, or destitute, or in danger, or threatened with death? (As the Scriptures say, 'For your sake we are killed every day; we are being slaughtered like sheep.') No, despite all these things, overwhelming victory is ours through Christ, who loved us" (Romans 8:35–37 NLT).

Reflect

Loss. It hurts just to say it. We all experience loss. Some experience the loss of a game, whereas others experience the loss of a child. Those are two extremes of loss are difficult to compare. Loss has different degrees of intensity, but the result is the same—a feeling of hurt and emptiness. Let's unwrap the feelings that accompany loss. When you hurt, how do you deal with it? Some pout, others withdraw from people and build invisible walls around themselves, and still others try to hurt someone else, thinking it will take away their own hurt. Hurting others or withdrawing does not make hurt go away. It only leads to more isolation at the time when you really need someone who understands. When you hurt is not the time to run from love. Instead, it is the time to run to love.

When we suffer a loss, we can feel empty. We have given something a big place in our lives, and when it is gone we feel empty. Remember that God has said He will never forsake us

(Hebrews 13:5) and that nothing can separate us from His love (Romans 8:38). Perhaps if we build our life around knowing Him, the emptiness of loss will not last long and could be replaced by the comfort and encouragement that comes from knowing the One who will never leave us when we feel empty.

Respond
What have you lost? A game? Self-respect? A dream? Hope? A friend? A family member? How will you respond when you suffer a loss? First, realize that you do not have to go through this time alone. There are those who can help. Reach out to them. Do not push them away. Second, realize that God may be using this time for you to reach out to Him. He is faithful and still has a plan for your life.

Remember
Regardless of your loss, you can be more than victorious through Him who loves you and will never abandon you.

Praying

Read

"One day Jesus was praying in a certain place. When he finished, one of his disciples said to him, 'Lord, teach us to pray'" (Luke 11:1 NIV).

Reflect

Praying has been a part of humanity since the beginning of humankind. The Old Testament records that after the prophet Elijah prayed, fire came down from heaven. Daniel prayed to understand the king's dream, and Jonah prayed from the belly of a great fish. People pray for many reasons. We often pray because we want God to intervene in our circumstances. Or we might pray because want to hear from Him. Regardless of the motivation to pray, Jesus says you can connect with God in heaven.

Jesus' disciples wanted to learn how to pray. They must have seen Jesus's connection with the heavenly Father and they wanted it as well. One of the things they must have noticed about His prayer life was that *He was praying in a certain place.* He obviously had a dedicated place, and dedicated time that He spent with the Father. He made it a priority to pull away from the crowds and activity of the world so He could focus on the Father and bring the issues of the day to Him.

Respond

The disciples had a great idea when they asked Jesus to teach them to pray. Perhaps that is where you should start. Ask Him to teach you. Jesus gave His disciples an outline to follow when they prayed. First, recognize where God is, that is, in heaven, which means He has an entirely different perspective on your situation. Second, honor God's name. His name is special and should never be misused or taken lightly. Rather, it should be revered. Third, acknowledge His program and plan (His kingdom and His will) and declare its accomplishment as your first priority. Fourth, ask Him to give you the things you need to accomplish His plan today. Ask Him to forgive the times you have ignored Him and His plan and program, and stop and forgive those who have sinned against you. Finally, ask Him to keep you away from the things that can lead to you sinning and to rescue you from sinful traps. End by reminding Him that you know it is all about Him and not about you.

Remember

Praying like Jesus prayed can lead to living like Jesus lived.

Putting Action into Your Prayers

Read

"But we prayed to our God and posted a guard day and night to meet this threat" (Nehemiah 4:9 NIV).

Reflect

For a person to be successful, he or she must strike a balance between praying and planning. The opposition against Nehemiah was intensifying. Therefore, his praying had to intensify. Not only did Nehemiah intensify the prayer time, but also he put his prayers into action by setting up a guard to watch the enemy. Some were kneelers and some were squealers. Some prayed and some watched. But all took part in carrying out God's plan to rebuild the wall.

Can you see this happening? Nehemiah hears the opposition. He sees them beef up their troops. What's a leader to do? He says, "Come on, boys. Let's get on our knees and ask God how we should handle this opposition. But while we pray, some of you watch the enemy and let us know what they're doing." Nehemiah was a man of prayer *and* action. In today's verse, Nehemiah shows us how faith and action are to be linked together. In the New Testament, James puts it this way: "For without action, faith is dead" (James 2:17). This principle came into play for Nehemiah just as it would for us today. To demonstrate our faith, we need to have action plans.

Respond

Some people claim to have great faith, but they don't *do* anything to promote their faith. Therefore, their faith is questionable. God wants us not only to pray, but also to act on our prayers. When we have a word from God, it is as good as gold and we must act on it.

Have you been listening to God speak to you lately about the action He wants you to take in serving Him? What have you done with His instructions to you? Take a minute or two right now to seek His input on the issue of your service. Ask Him to reveal to you where He wants you to put your faith into action in the body of Christ. But while you pray, set up a watch over your heart to look out for the enemy of convenient excuses that is out to destroy your service before you even start. Spend some quality time with God right now.

Remember

Action plans authenticate faith.

Spiritual Birthdays

Read
"Yet to all who did receive him, to those who believed in his name, he gave the right to become children of God" (John 1:12 NIV).

Reflect
June 14. June 16. June 17. December 19. Those are special days in the Hufty household. It was on those special days that each one of our family members was born again. Each one of us came into the world in different years and in different settings, and different influences impacted us. We each individually came to know God through the grace of His Son, Jesus.

Respond
Because these days are special, we Huftys celebrate—with a big cookie cake. At the end of the special day, we all sit around the table and talk about why this day was so special. For example, my son, Zac, made his commitment to Christ on June 14. On June 14, we place the cookie on the table with the icing lettering reading "Happy Spiritual Birthday," and we say, "Tell us about it, Zac." He says something like, "Well, remember we were at camp, and after the service I told Mom I wanted to become a Christian, and she said 'We can talk about it later.' And then I went to you and said I wanted to become a Christian, and you said, 'Let's talk about it later.' And finally I said, 'If you won't lead me to Christ, I am going to find someone who will.' And then, remember, we

went downstairs in that big room and sat on those metal chairs, and it was there I asked Jesus to come into my heart and forgive me of my sin, and I told Him I would do my best to live for Him." We sit and eat that sweet cookie and listen to that sweet story of how a tender heart responded to a compelling attraction to the Savior. We do this every year on June 14. We remember the day Zac was born again. It was real!

Why do we need to be intentional about remembering? Because we, like the children of Israel, have a propensity to forget. We need to realize there will be days when He will not seem real. Therefore, we need to put milestones and reminders in place so we can remember when we knew He was real. If we don't, we will forget His goodness, His faithfulness, and His mighty acts of love. How tragic to forget.

Remember
If you know Him, you need to celebrate and remember.

The Living Word of God

Read

"For the word of God is alive and active. Sharper than any double-edged sword, it penetrates even to dividing soul and spirit, joints and marrow; it judges the thoughts and attitudes of the heart" (Hebrews 4:12 NIV).

Reflect

I remember as a small boy playing outside our country church after services. I would hear my dad call me to come to the car so we could go home, but sometimes I continued to play with my friends. After a minute or two, he would call again—"Tom, come on, we're leaving"—but I continued to play. The third time, my dad would raise his voice (disciplining by decibel) and say, "Leslie Thomas Hufty, get over here right now. We are leaving!" It was at that point I raced over to him. Before I got in the car, he asked me, "Son, did you hear me call you the first two times?" "Yes, sir," I replied. He said, "Then why didn't you come?" I said, "Because, Daddy, you didn't use your loud voice."

Sometimes God uses His loud voice too. Sometimes He uses a still, small voice (1 Kings 19:11–18). But regardless of His tone, His objective is to get us to listen to Him. However, I am afraid that sometimes we go through the motions of listening but that our listening is never translated into obedience.

Hebrews 4:12 reminds us that God's Word has a dynamic to it that no other piece of literature has. It is alive. It produces action. There is one thing we can bank on when we proclaim God's Word to someone: it will always make an impact on the listener. God's Word has been affecting people's lives for centuries and will continue to do so. How is it affecting your life today?

Respond

Are you like I was when my dad was calling me, waiting for the disciplinary voice before I obeyed? Are you distracted from His Word by being friendly with the things of this world, or do you just not listen at all? The truth is, God is speaking and we all need to listen.

Remember

God will speak if you will listen. He is never too busy for you.

The Scarlet Cord

Read

"The men said to her, 'This oath you made us swear will not be binding on us unless, when we enter the land, you have tied this scarlet cord in the window through which you let us down, and unless you have brought your father and mother, your brothers and all your family into your house'" (Joshua 2:17–18 NIV).

Reflect

"Okay, guys, remember that when you see the scarlet cord hanging out the window, you should protect that place, because the one who lives there protected us." The marching orders were clear. Jericho would fall, but one spot to be spared would be marked—Rahab's place. How would it be marked? With the scarlet cord.

At the time, Rahab probably did not fully understand the significance of that scarlet rope hanging out her window. But it was more than a signal of her location; it was an act of faith. She knew Jericho would fall. Her life would never be the same. She would never have the same neighbors, never live in the same place, never worship any other gods (she was a Canaanite, and they worshipped several gods), and never be outside of God's protection again. The scarlet rope hanging out her window was a sign that she believed God to be God.

Rahab put aside all her Canaanite gods for the one true God, whom she would grow to know much more intimately in the future. How surprised she would be to realize that someday this

God would enable her to get her life back together in such a way that she and her loved ones would become a major part of the Jewish family. Her name would go down in history as a prostitute saved by the grace of God. She also would be remembered as one of the world's most unusual mothers. She was the mother of Boaz, which made her the great-great-grandmother of King David, one of the direct ancestors of Joseph, who was the husband of Mary, the mother of Jesus.

Respond
Hanging the scarlet rope from her window was risky for Rahab, but she knew the only way life would get any better was to exercise some faith. Are you there? Do you need to exercise some faith? Do you need to throw a scarlet rope out the window of your life?

Remember
Exercise faith and God will move on your behalf.

Meaning

When you understand the reason you are here, your decisions will have conviction, your direction will be clear, and your destiny will be your quest.

"A life devoted to things is a dead life, a stump; a God-shaped life is a flourishing tree" (Proverbs 11:28 MSG).

Touching a Day You Will Never See

Read

"Start children off on the way they should go, and even when they are old they will not turn from it" (Proverbs 22:6 NIV).

Reflect

Several years ago I was making an entry in my daily journal. I remember how blessed I felt to be a father to and parent of two adorable children. I think they were around four and eight years old at the time. I wondered how good of a parent I would be. I had great parents but was afraid that the trend might skip a generation and I might not have what it took to love my children and train them in the way they should go. One thought continued to come to my mind as I prayed for them. Here is that phrase as I recorded it in my journal that morning: "They will touch a day I will never see; I pray they make it brighter."

Not long after I wrote that entry, my wife, Rhonda, was reading it. She has such a creative mind. She immediately thought of a picture she had taken a few years before of our children standing on the beach, holding hands, and watching the sunrise. Her imaginative skills went into action and she had the picture blown up and framed with the phrase from my journal etched in the matting.

Our kids are adults now. They both have children of their own. To this day that picture hangs over my desk in my office, reminding me of what my life is all about. Touching a day I will never see is what I live for every day. The words I say, the random acts of kindness God's hand moves me to do (for I would not do them on my own), are the result of a passion He has placed in me. Every child I see in church running down the hall with arms open wide to hug me is like medicine to my soul.

Respond
Children grow up. The way we are wired and the influences we allow in our lives shape who we become. The beautiful thing about that shaping is that during childhood, the clay of our character is much more moldable. The cast of our hearts when we are children is more flexible because we haven't yet aged and experienced the cruel hammers of the world system.

Remember
You can impact tomorrow by loving and influencing a child today.

The Things That Last Forever

"But now abide faith, hope, love, these three: but the greatest of these is love" (1 Corinthians 13:13 NIV).

Reflect
There is a story that circulated through history about the great French leader Napoleon Bonaparte. His leadership was beginning to fade when he invaded Russia. History tells us that during this invasion, Napoleon became so concerned about his position back in France that he left the French army and returned to France with a few other men. Arriving at a river crossing, he asked the ferryman if many deserters had come that way. The ferryman replied, "No, you are the first." Ouch. Bonaparte's leadership was waning, and yet his compatriots continued to follow their failing leader.

As believers, we have a leader that will never fail. All we have done for Him will never be in vain and will be rewarded. "For the Son of Man is going to come in his Father's glory with his angels, and then he will reward each person according to what he has done" (Matthew 16:27). So the questions are as follows: What have you done? What have you given that will result in a reward? But that is really not the point, is it? We do not give just because He has promised a reward. We give because He *is* our reward! He has impacted our life so much that for us to give is a natural response to His supernatural love.

Even though many things do not last long, God's Word guarantees us at least one thing—God's love will last forever. Psalm 136 tells us over and over that His love endures forever. There is nothing we can do that will ever make His love fade away.

Respond
Just think, all the things you will ever possess in your lifetime will someday come to nothing. All you have ever worked for will pass away. But God's love for you will never fade away. How does that make you feel? Does it stir up in you a desire to be all you can be for Him? To know that you will have God's undying love forever is a great motivation to please Him every day.

Remember
You are the object of His love.

The Joy of Common Values

Read

"Then make my joy complete by being like-minded, having the same love, being of one spirit and purpose" (Philippians 2:2 NIV).

Reflect

My wife and I read many of the same books. We don't necessarily have the same taste in books, but we agreed a long time ago to read much of the same material. The reason is simple: when we read the same books, we get on the same page. We have great discussions, we share opinions and values, and we begin to think alike in the important areas of our relationship.

Do you know someone who thinks like you do, I mean, someone you can be in a conversation with and know what he or she is going to say before he or she says it? How does that happen? Usually it happens because you have spent time with the person, you have shared with him or her, he or she has shared with you, and you know his or her way of thinking. Thought patterns are so important when it comes to friendships. The more that friends think alike on important things, the deeper the friendship can grow and the more joy can be experienced through the friendship. Of course, your thoughts will not be identical to anyone else's. But when it comes to important things like love, attitudes, and purpose, friendships can grow deep when friends are like-minded.

Nothing is more important than relationships and purpose in life. Your meaning in life is amplified by those relationships you build with friends who share your common values and purpose. If you build deep friendships with people who do not share your values in life, your purpose for living will become foggy and confused. You will become like the person James mentions, "a double-minded man, unstable in all he does" (James 1:8). Paul found strength from his friends in Philippi who shared his purpose. This resulted in an experience of joy even while he was imprisoned.

Respond

Do you know the purpose for your life? Is that purpose to know God and share His love? If you take that as your purpose statement, do you have close friends who help you fulfill that purpose for your life?

Take a moment or two right now to praise and thank God for His wonderful love. Ask Him to forgive you for the times in the past twenty-four hours that you have ignored His purpose for your life and disobeyed Him. Finally, pray that God will provide friends who will strengthen your walk with Him.

Remember

Be like-minded with God.

The Grace of Fear

Read

"Jonah began by going a day's journey into the city, proclaiming, 'Forty more days and Nineveh will be overthrown.' The Ninevites believed God" (Jonah 3:4–5a NIV).

Reflect

God knows what buttons to push to get our attention. Nineveh was one of the most violent cities in all of history. The torturous deaths that Ninevites inflicted on their enemies were unmatched. They brought persecution to a new level with impalings, beheadings, and skinning people alive. Their reputation for violence was unrivaled, and the atrocities they committed were unparalleled. Yet the God of grace sent them a prophet with news that they had met their match. It was a simple message: "Forty more days and Nineveh will be overthrown." And for some reason, they listened. Not only did they listen, but also they believed and were terrified—and their king proclaimed a fast for everyone to observe in hope that God would relent and spare them. When God saw their acts of repentance, He showed mercy, extended His grace, and let them live. What motivated their repentance? Fear.

I especially love the second verse of John Newton's hymn "Amazing Grace." Do you remember it? "'Twas grace that taught my heart to fear, and grace my fears relieved." God's grace can take the form of fear sometimes in order to connect to your heart. Fear is a strong motivator. God knew that if the people of

Nineveh were presented with the choice of repenting or dying, their fear of death would result in action.

Respond

There are two ways to look at fear. We are not to fear humankind, but we are to fear God. Godly fear is healthy, because it can move us toward Him and away from our own destructive patterns. The fear of humankind often derails our purpose in life and our trust in God. It can take us down a path of defeat.

So where have you placed your fear? "The fear of the Lord is the beginning of wisdom" (Proverbs 9:10). If you learn to fear the Lord, you may better understand His amazing grace.

Remember

Godly fear moves us away from sin and closer to Him.

The Aerial View

Read

"Now the Lord is the Spirit, and where the Spirit of the Lord is, there is freedom" (2 Corinthians 3:17 NIV).

Reflect

There is an old story about a fly that was circling above a circus of fellow flies below. He saw the other flies dancing on a piece of paper and appearing to have a good time. Just at that moment he whizzed by a spider and heard the spider say, "Boy, it sure looks like they're having fun down there. You better join them before the party is over." The fly was hesitant, but the spider continued to persuade him by pointing out how he was missing out on all the fun that his friends were obviously having without him. After a moment or two, the fly swooped down and landed next to one of his friends, where he stayed—and died. What appeared to be true wasn't true at all. What looked like freedom and fun was slavery and bondage. From a distance the dance floor looked harmless, but a closer look revealed that the dance floor was really flypaper.

The great influencers of today's culture—media, music, and entertainment—condone the dance floor. They create a visual that appears to be filled with pleasure. Everybody is doing it. Most seem to be having fun. However, all that the culture reveals to us is the aerial view, where it looks like everyone is having fun and there are no consequences for irresponsible behavior. The seducing arm of our culture is powerful. Unfortunately, oftentimes we are unprepared and vulnerable, not realizing that we are the targets of this aggressive worldly mind-set.

Respond

Where are you in this metaphoric scenario? Are you flying above? Are you flying low? Are you listening to the spider (today's cultural influencers)? Or are you already stuck on the dance floor? No matter where you are in the picture, you need to be rescued. The Scripture tells us there is freedom in the Spirit. That means when you trust God with your life, you can fly in freedom, because you are taking your cues from the One who knows the culture and its strategy. When you follow His lead, He can keep you free from the cultural tricks that sidetrack you from your purpose in life.

Remember

True freedom is only found in Christ.

Taking a Close Look at Me

Read

"'Woe to me!' I cried. 'I am ruined! For I am a man of unclean lips and I live among a people of unclean lips, and my eyes have seen the King, the Lord Almighty'" (Isaiah 6:5 NIV).

Reflect

When Isaiah saw the Lord like he had never seen Him before, something very interesting happened: he saw himself and how sinful he was. When you see God for who He is, seeing yourself for who you are becomes a glaring reality. When Isaiah saw how pure God was, he immediately realized how impure and unholy he was. He saw his sin like never before. He took the closest look possible at his own life and saw that he was a "man of unclean lips." Perhaps he had been dishonest and told lies. Perhaps he had been critical and sarcastic, tearing others down. Perhaps he cussed like a drunken sailor. We don't know the specifics, but we do know that the sin he was referring to was keeping him from living out God's purpose for his life. He needed help.

There are many ways our mouth can hurt our relationship with God. But it wasn't just Isaiah's unclean lips that hurt his relationship with God; he had another problem. He hung out with people who were just like him. Did Isaiah influence them or did they influence him? One thing for sure, you are known by the company you keep, and you don't become more pure and holy hanging around those who are impure and unholy.

Respond

When Isaiah saw his sin, God willingly made provision for him to be cleansed from his sin. When you are cleansed from your sin, you position yourself in such a way that God can work through your life. To have a fresh encounter with God, cleansing must take place first. God desires not to bless our sin but to cleanse us from it. We need to be like the psalmist and ask God to search us and see if there is any unclean way in us, so that we can be cleansed and commit ourselves to a faithful relationship with Him (Psalm 139:23–24). How long has it been since you have taken a close look at yourself?

Take some time today to praise and thank God for His willingness to forgive your sin. Ask God to examine you and reveal to you all the sin in your life. Then confess to Him and experience His forgiveness. Trust Him for His forgiveness.

Remember

There is nothing He can't forgive.

Security for the Future

Read

"And if I go and prepare a place for you, I will come back and take you to be with me that you also may be where I am" (John 14:3 NIV).

Reflect

God not only has a purpose for your life here and now, but He also has a plan for your future. The future is a scary thing if you do not have any security. So, what were the disciples to think about their future when Jesus said He was leaving? Obviously their hearts sank. But Jesus gave them a promise and a hope for the future. He said, " I will come back and take you with me." You have the same promise. When it seems your situation is hopeless, remember, He is coming back. It's not over.

Because we have the certainty of His death and resurrection, our hope is not in vain. His return is inevitable. Why? Because truth characterized His entire life while He was on the earth. Everything He said would happen did happen. Therefore, based on Jesus's track record, our hope is sure. He will return and take us to be with Him. Whether we go to heaven through the valley of the shadow of death or are still alive when He returns, our future is secure—it is based on His Word.

Respond

Heaven is a place of love and joy. Scripture tells us it is a place devoid of sorrow, death, pain, crying, and night. It is the place where there is no need for the sun, for the glory of God illuminates its expanse. Heaven is a place where we will be reunited with those we love who know Him. Heaven is also a place where you will be rewarded for your faith. It is the dwelling place of God and will soon be your dwelling place if you have committed your life to Him through Jesus Christ. Who would not want to be there? Yet many today ignore the future reality of heaven because they are blinded by the world system. If you live like you are going to heaven, you can point out the way to others so that they may get there.

Are the people you love going to be in heaven? Are there people in your life whom you would be disappointed not to find in heaven? Pray for those folks today.

Remember
Your future is secure if you have given your life to Christ.

Hufty Holiday

Read

"When the Lord your God brings you into the land he swore to your fathers ... a land with large, flourishing cities you did not build, houses filled with all kinds of good things you did not provide, wells you did not dig, and vineyards and olive groves you did not plant—then when you eat and are satisfied, be careful that you do not forget the Lord, who brought you out of Egypt, out of the land of slavery" (Deuteronomy 6:10–12 NIV).

Reflect

When I was a kid, my family would celebrate what we called "Hufty holidays." These were days we set aside for the family to get away from the hustle and bustle of life and just enjoy each other. We would take a break from the routine and remind ourselves what it meant to be a Hufty. Sometimes you can forget what your life is about when you are immersed in the rat race of the world system.

I'm happy to say that my family has continued this tradition, passing it on even today. In fact, the phrase *Hufty holiday* is one of the favorite sayings in our family. The challenge is that our kids wanted to celebrate Hufty holidays often—and on regular school days.

Holidays are holy days. They are days when we stop and remember what is important. One of the reasons for holidays is that God doesn't want us to get 365 days away from remembering what He has done. He wants us to have regular times of renewal because we need them. He knows that if we don't set aside time to remember Him, we will fall into the trap of the world's mindset and not acknowledge Him in our everyday lives.

Respond

How do you think you can avoid forgetting God in your daily life? First, make a big deal about salvation. Try to remember the day you became a Christian, and celebrate it as your spiritual birthday. If you can't remember the exact date, choose a day and make it a celebration. Do the same thing for your family members. Take them out to eat and talk about all the events that led to their spiritual birth. Whatever you do, make it memorable. Second, retell the old stories of how God worked in the lives of His people. Recall the events and prayers that were involved. Remind your family that the God of the past is still God today.

Remember

Don't forget God in your daily life, and don't forget to surprise your family with a "holiday" in your future.

In All Things at All Times

Read

"And God is able to make all grace abound to you, so that in all things at all times, having all that you need, you will abound in every good work" (2 Corinthians 9:8 NIV).

Reflect

Soviet Pastor Richard Wurmbrand, the author of *Tortured for Christ*, suffered terribly for his faith in God. Yet he said that even while in prison, he saw fellow Soviet believers practice generous giving. "When we were given one slice of bread a week and dirty soup every day, we decided we would faithfully 'tithe' even then. Every tenth week we took the slice of bread and gave it to the weaker brothers as our tithe to the Master" (Richard Wurmbrand, *Tortured for Christ* [Bartlesville, OK: Living Sacrifice Book Company, 1998.] 38).

Before Pastor Wurmbrand was ever imprisoned, Paul wrote these words to the believers at Corinth: "And God is able to make all grace abound to you, so that in all things at all times, having all that you need, you will abound in every good work." Paul knew what it was like to feel the treatment received in prison, for he was imprisoned—and while incarcerated he continued to work for the Lord. Even today, we as believers memorize the words he wrote from inside a harsh prison cell. God truly did make all grace abound to him so that, even in prison, he could abound in every good work.

Respond

The good work that God wants you to do is to make Him look good in every area of your life—social, physical, mental, spiritual, and financial. Regardless of your situation, God's grace is abounding to you so that in all things at all times He may provide all that you need to produce good works. For that Soviet pastor, it was a piece of bread. For many of us, it is much, much more.

Take inventory right now of the things God has given you. How are you using those things to abound in good works? Are you just letting His gifts sit around, or are you using them to bring joy to another? Thank God today for the way He has blessed you. Then ask Him to give you the strength and courage and creativity to use all that stuff He has given you to produce good works and to benefit others.

Remember

God is faithful all the time.

Reaping the Measure You Sow

Read

"Remember this: Whoever sows sparingly will also reap sparingly, and whoever sows generously will also reap generously" (2 Corinthians 9:6 NIV).

Reflect

Having been raised on a farm, I can fully understand the principle of reaping what you sow. If my dad went out to plant corn and only put a few seeds of corn in the ground, we could expect only a small amount of corn to be harvested. But if he put a lot in the ground, we could expect a lot in return. The same is true of the Lord's work—the more generous you are in planting yourself in His work, the more you can expect in return.

If you understand the grace of God, then giving becomes a part of who you are and not just something you do. A giving life is a meaningful life. Those who are givers know that giving is a natural part of being a Christian. When you give, you experience something inside that is tremendously satisfying. The fact that you receive blessings from God is simply a fringe benefit of giving. The blessings you receive may not be material, but remember, you cannot out give God.

Respond

The opposite of being generous is being selfish. Selfishness comes naturally to all of us, whereas generosity has to be practiced in order to become a habit. But being generous is a big deal to God.

He is concerned about what you do with what He gives you. Many people want God to give them more money so they can buy more stuff. However, God is more concerned about what we are doing with all the things we have that money can't buy.

Being generous is one of the reasons you are here. Is *generous* a word that accurately describes you? Or do you sow sparingly? Take some time right now to praise and thank God for all He has given to you that money cannot buy—stuff like trusting relationships, spiritual gifts, good health, friends, a good church, etc. Ask Him to forgive you for the times when you have been blinded by what you don't have to the point that you've neglected to appreciate all the things you do have. Now take a moment to pray for those you know who are in need. Ask God to give you a generous spirit in order to minister to them.

Remember
We all reap what we sow.

Press On

Read

"Not that I have already obtained all this, or have already been made perfect, but I press on to take hold of that for which Christ Jesus took hold of me" (Philippians 3:12 NIV).

Reflect

Why do you exist? What is your meaning in life? These are great questions. When you discover the answer, it clears a lot of clutter out of your life. It helps you make better choices and helps you control your involvements. Many people go through life with no idea of why God put them here. They do not live on purpose. They live on their own perspective. But God has another perspective about their lives. He has a plan for each of us. The apostle Paul had discovered that plan.

Even though Paul's life was not easy, he said, "I press on." To him, life was not life unless it was being lived according to the plan God had laid out for him. Paul believed that unless his purpose in life was being fulfilled, his life was meaningless. He did not let prison walls or Roman law limit the fulfilling of God's purpose in his life. Every day his mind was focused on how he could implement his reason for existence in his daily activities. In fact, because of his commitment to God's purpose for his life, being surrounded by prison walls only increased his effectiveness.

Just like Paul, you have a call on your life. Jesus has called you to follow His plan, to be a minister where you are, and to fulfill His purpose on this earth. Take a good look at Jesus's life and see what He has called you to do. He was a model of pressing on. Are you finding it difficult to follow Him fully in your daily life? Press on. He is with you, supporting you.

Respond

Have you lost sight of God's purpose for your life? Are you anywhere close to reflecting Him to a world that doesn't know Him? Press on. Are you facing difficult times? Is it tough to hold onto your sanity? Press on! Do you feel like you're alone in this life? Are you just going through the motions without hope? Press on! He is there for you. His purpose hasn't changed, and His enthusiasm about your life is still strong.

Remember

Regardless of the circumstances or feelings, press on!

Practice until You Are Productive

Read

"For though by this time you ought to be teachers, you have need again for someone to teach you the elementary principles of the oracles of God, and you have come to need milk and not solid food" (Hebrews 5:12 NASB).

Reflect

He was a student I had in college who had the talent that few had. I saw him do things on the basketball court that one only sees in NBA highlight films. He was incredible, but for some reason he never went on to make it in the big time. He had the skills, but there was something missing inside that prohibited him from getting to the next level of competition. Was the missing thing confidence? I think that had something to do with it. But it was more than that. His talent could have taken him to a much higher level of play, but his drive to do things he didn't feel comfortable doing kept him on the playground, playing in pickup games.

Have you ever met someone who had incredible potential but, because there was something broken inside of that person, he or she never reached it? Because of the person's unwillingness to practice the difficult things, he or she never realized his or her potential. He or she decided to be content to play in the playground of mediocrity rather than push him- or herself to practice the things that pay off in productivity.

You have great potential, but potential means nothing if it does not lead to production. Jesus said that we are to bear fruit. We are to be productive. As we mature as believers, the fruit we produce becomes second nature for us and noticeable to others. Our "fruit" will be the evidence to others that we belong to Him. For us, the fruit we produce will be evidence that God is in the process of helping us realize our potential.

Respond

The writer of Hebrews was telling his audience that they had been believers long enough to have started sharing their faith with others. But instead they were still acting like spiritual babies. They were going through a second childhood. Therefore, they needed someone to teach them again how to grow. They had potential to bear a lot of fruit, but they were not being productive with what they knew.

Remember

God wants to help you realize your full potential in a way that will help others.

Pottery Plans

Read

"So I went down to the potter's house and saw him working at the potter's wheel. He was using his hands to make a pot from clay, but something went wrong with it. So he used that clay to make another pot the way he wanted it to be" (Jeremiah 18:3–4 NCV).

Reflect

When I was dating the woman who is now my wife, Rhonda, I was at her house quite a bit. At the time, her mom was in school studying to be an art teacher. Art was one thing I had nothing in common with my future mother-in-law. One evening she invited the family and some of her colleagues who were professional artists to sit around the kitchen table and work with clay. We were instructed to make whatever came to our mind. My mind was totally blank. I set there and stared at my lifeless clump of clay. The others moved their clay with precision. I patted my bump of dirt like it was a pet. Out of desperation I peeked at the other artists' work, hoping I might find some inspiration. Did it help? No. I couldn't see what they could see as they worked with the clay. So, what was I to do? I did what any frustrated, intimidated, inartistic person would do in that setting: I took my thumb and pushed it as far as I could into the mass of clay. Guess what happened next? Those artists started looking at my clay. "Hey, that's nice. What are you going to do with that?" I responded, "Well, all I can do with it." I had no idea what to do with it! Do you know what happened to that chunk of clay? Rhonda's mom took it, turned it into a beautiful piece of art, presented it in class as her project, and received an A on it.

Respond

Our lives are not in the hands of some invisible force or subject to blind fate. They are in the hands of a person, Almighty God, the Master Potter. He has a personal concern for our lives. He has a vision for what we can be. The question is, will we be moldable clay in His hands or will we harden our hearts and resist His work?

Remember

The Master Potter has something beautiful in mind for you. If you are moldable, He can make you into a masterpiece.

Passing on the Legacy

Read

"Tell them that the flow of the Jordan was cut off before the ark of the covenant of the Lord. When it crossed the Jordan, the waters of the Jordan were cut off. These stones are to be a memorial to the people of Israel forever" (Joshua 4:7 NIV).

Reflect

There is an old story about a little girl who asked her mom why she always cut off the end of the ham before she put it in the oven to cook. The mother replied, "That's what my mom used to do, and the ham always tasted delicious." So, the little girl asked her grandmother why she cut off the end of the ham before she put it in the oven to cook. The grandmother replied, "That's what my mother always did, and it tasted so good." Finally, the little girl went to her great-grandmother and asked the same question. "Why did you always cut the end of the ham off before you put it in the oven to cook?" Her great-grandmother looked at her and said, "Well, sweetheart, my pan was too short to hold the whole ham. I had to cut the end off to make it fit."

Do you have family traditions that you don't understand? God was instructing Joshua to establish a method by which He would be remembered by the future generations of Israel. When an Israelite family was on vacation and they passed the pile of stones on the bank of the Jordan and a child asked, why the stones were there, it would present a golden opportunity to pass on the legacy of how God delivered His people that day. The parent could tell the child that the stones were carried out of the river bottom while the waters were held back and the nation of Israel passed by the Ark of the Covenant.

Respond
Does your family have any special memories of God working in their life? What family traditions does your family have to pass on to future generations? Family traditions are special. They are even more special when they point to a way that God has worked in your life.

Remember
The most important legacy you leave is the one that points those who follow you to Jesus.

Only One Way

Read

"But as many as received Him, to them He gave the right to become children of God, even to those who believe in His name" (John 1:12 NIV).

Reflect

On October 25, 1964, the Minnesota Vikings' defensive lineman Jim Marshall collected a fumble and ran the ball into the end zone. The only problem was that he ran to the wrong end zone. Instead of scoring what he thought was a touchdown for his team, he scored a safety against his own team. As he ran the wrong way, his teammates were jumping up and down screaming at him. He thought they were cheering him on, but they were trying to stop him from making a big mistake that would be on the bloopers highlight films for years to come. He could have argued that it was pretty narrow-minded of the rules and the referees to only allow a team to run in one direction, but the rules were established to provide enjoyment and prevent chaos during the game. Therefore, Marshall was stuck with the embarrassment, because the rules had to be enforced.

The same principle is true in regard to spirituality. To be able to enter into God's heaven, you must be born again. There is no other way. You must *receive* Jesus as your personal Lord and Savior. The Scripture is not narrow-minded. It is simply the truth as God has established it.

Many people today believe that if they merely live a good life, they will be able to enter into heaven. But that is not true. That is a human-made philosophy that will lead many astray. If one could enter heaven by being good, then why would Jesus have had to die? Your salvation came at a great price: the death of God's only Son. He died so you could be born into His family by accepting and receiving Him into your life.

Respond
If you have never asked Christ to come into your life and take control, now would be a great time to do that. Ask Him to come into your life and forgive you of your sins. If you are sincere, at that instant you will be born into the family of God.

Remember
There are a lot of wrong ways in life, but there is only one way to heaven.

Minimizing God

Read

"You must not make for yourself an idol of any kind or an image of anything in the heavens or on the earth or in the sea" (Exodus 20:4 NLT).

Reflect

You may say, "I have never been tempted to break this commandment. I have never once tried to make an idol to put on my mantle and to worship. I have obeyed this one. The others, maybe not so much, but I am not crafty or skilled with tools; therefore, I am clean when it comes to this one."

Literally speaking, you are probably safe. You probably have never made a graven image or bowed down to an idol. But the commandment goes much deeper than that. In fact, when you try to reduce God in any way or give your affection to something or someone else above Him, you are breaking this commandment.

Because God made human beings, He understood the children of Israel thoroughly. He knew their propensity to worship whatever seemed to work. Worship for many of them was relative. If they needed rain, they would worship the rain god. If there was a famine, they would worship whatever god that claimed to provide what they needed. He also knew that worshipping a God they did not see was a major frustration for His people, especially when neighboring countries worshipped gods (i.e., idols) that could be seen.

In contrast to the worship practices of the heathen nations, God commanded that we not only worship Him and Him alone but also that we never craft anything that in any way, shape, or form represents Him. Anything that humankind can manufacture will never be able to represent accurately who God is. He refuses to be diminished down to a hand-made trinket as was done by the heathen nations that manufactured their own gods, making them in their own image.

Respond
God made us in His own image, not the other way around. He is not a policeman in the sky or a vending machine that produces blessings at our will. When we reduce Him in our lives, we have not only an inaccurate perception of who He is but also an erroneous view of who we are and who He desires for us to be. Don't miss His big-picture vision for your life by minimizing who He is in your mind.

Remember
Refuse to reduce God.

It Is Not I

Read

"I know that the Lord has given this land to you and that a great fear of you has fallen on us, so that all who live in this country are melting in fear because of you" (Joshua 2:9 NIV).

Reflect

There is a story told by the British Baptist pastor Charles H. Spurgeon about the great theologian Augustine following the latter's conversion to Christianity. One day after his conversion to Christ, Augustine was walking down a street. Coming toward him was a prostitute, a woman with whom he was all too familiar. She was smiling, as she assumed Augustine had returned to his former life after having gone through his little religious phase. As they approached each other, Augustine kept his eyes focused straight ahead and never looked at the prostitute as he passed her. After they had passed each other, she turned and called his name. "Augustine." She said, "It is I," mentioning her name. Augustine stopped, turned to her, and said, "But it is not I."

God had made an impact on Rahab the prostitute. She was one of the most unlikely people for God to use to bring a great victory for His people. But we must remember that God uses the unlikely to accomplish His purposes in order that He may be recognized as the One who is accomplishing the work. Rahab was no longer a woman who was ignoring God. In fact, because of her acts of faith in protecting the spies, God promised to rescue her when Jericho fell—and He made good on that promise.

God is looking to use those who will listen to Him and seek Him with all of their heart. It makes no difference what you have done in the past or, worse yet, what you have become. All that matters is your willingness to be cleansed and used by Him now.

Respond
Have you had the same kind of experience Augustine had? When failures from your past revisit you, do you keep your focus straight in resistance to the temptations? Pray that God would place a hedge of protection around you so you may be a stronger witness for Him. Pray that when temptation comes your way, God would strengthen you to avoid a possible fall.

Remember
When God forgives, He forgives all our sin, past, present, and future.

His Invitation to Follow His Commands

Read

"In the future, when your son asks you, 'What is the meaning of the stipulations, decrees and laws the Lord our God has commanded you?' tell him; 'We were slaves of Pharaoh in Egypt, but the Lord brought us out with a mighty hand'" (Deuteronomy 6:20 NIV).

Reflect

Rules seem to get a bad rap in our culture. We complain that they are too binding, too restrictive, and a downright pain. We bend them, stretch them, and break them. We quote little sayings like "Rules were made to be broken." Why? Because we have the wrong idea about rules, especially God's rules, more commonly known as His commands.

God's commands were born out of His love. He loves us and does not want us to mess up our lives, so He gave us the Ten Commandments to follow. If we follow them, not only will we show our love for Him, but also His commands will protect us from messing up our lives.

Respond

The psalmist wrote in Psalm 1:2 that he delighted in the commands of the Lord. I wonder why? Could it have been that he had been burned by not obeying God's laws at one time and then he realized how much he would be protected if he followed them? Is that when he grew to love them? Perhaps. Or maybe he just loved the laws of the Lord because he loved the Lord. The question today is, do you love His commands or are they burdensome to you? He gave you His commands so you may live a fulfilled life and pass it on to your children. His commands are designed to provide you with a safe and fulfilling life and to protect you from making a mess of your life. Why not start loving His commands today? They will protect you!

In the New Testament, John connected this idea of God's love with His commands when he said, "In fact, this is love for God: to keep his commands. And his commands are not burdensome" (1 John 5:3 NIV). His commands were never designed to hurt you or be a burden to you. They were intended to help you. When you follow them, He will trust you with more of His will for you.

Remember
His commands are designed to protect you and provide for you.

Handling God's Assignments

Read

"Many are the plans in a man's heart, but it is the Lord's purpose that prevails" (Proverbs 19:21 NIV).

Reflect

As a young man I learned this word-picture from a wise mentor. He said, "There is nothing that has come into your life, or that will come into your life, that does not first pass through God's hands. None of the circumstances or challenges you are facing have sneaked by Him. In fact, as they passed through His hands He shaped them just for you." What a word-picture! God knows everything I am facing. In fact, He saw it coming before I did and He let it happen. It may not be what I planned, but He had it planned all along. Why? To accomplish His purpose in my life and through my life. I know He loves me; therefore, I know that when something comes my way, He has confidence it will eventually accomplish something positive in my life.

Part of the purpose of your life is to take the assignments God gives you and faithfully accomplish His purpose. If you are faithful to do the small things, He will give you greater responsibilities. Each one of these opportunities passes through His hands. They are tailor-made for you. He believes that through the personality and abilities He has given you, you are the person to accomplish His assigned task.

Respond

When the tornado of 2011 hit Joplin, Missouri, I immediately called a friend of mine who was a pastor there—first, to find out if he was all right, and second to see how I could help. He answered the phone and told me that he was fine, but then he made a statement that I will never forget. He said, "Tom, the Father has given us a new assignment." What a great perspective. God uses tough times in our lives to assign us a new task. Typically, the task will have two components: (1) to help someone and (2) to make Him look good. That church went on to minister to hundreds of people in need, all in the name of the One they love the most, Jesus. When you look at your crisis as His assignments for you, you will see the hand of God working.

Remember

He sees and knows everything you are going through. Trust Him to help you get through it.

God's Workplace—in You

Read

"For it is God who works in you to will and to act according to His good purpose" (Philippians 2:13 NIV).

Reflect

God takes pleasure in working through your life. To fulfill God's good purpose in your life you must allow Him to work in you. That means when He tells you to repent (turn away) from something you have been thinking or doing wrong, you do it. If you refuse to repent, His work in you stops—and so does the fulfillment of His purpose in your life. His workshop is your life, and when you allow Him to work, He can produce some miraculous things. But when you don't allow Him to work in His workshop—when you make Him sit and be quiet in His workshop—the tools He has given you get rusty and become useless.

There are conditions to having a joyful life. Joy can only exist where it is allowed to exist. It cannot reside with worry. True joy cannot live with disobedience. When you are disobedient, you may experience a false sense of joy, but it will be fleeting and will eventually result in pain and grief. God will not bless you with His joy if you are disobedient. King David found this to be true when he sinned and was caught. He pleaded with God to restore the joy he once had (Psalm 51). Sin steals joy from our lives, making it so that until we allow God the freedom to work out His purpose in our lives, all our efforts and goals come up empty.

Respond

How would you describe your life in the eyes of the Great Workman? Would you say you are being productive in His eyes, or are you becoming rusty and useless? Does He have free rein in the workshop of your life, using all your tools and your skill set, or are you refusing Him? God is patient, but don't try His patience. He has a purpose for your life and wants to fulfill it.

Thank God for His plans for you. Pray He will forgive you for the times you have refused Him. His forgiveness is available, immediate, and complete. Pray for His guidance today and for a sensitive and courageous heart to follow His lead.

Remember

God wants to work in and through you in order to accomplish His purpose in this world.

God Is Speaking; Will You Listen?

Read

"In the past God spoke to our forefathers through the prophets at many times and in various ways, but in these last days he has spoken to us by his Son" (Hebrews 1:1–2a NIV).

Reflect

Voices are interesting—unique, to say the least. God created each of us with a specific voice. I clearly remember my dad's voice booming from the stands when I played baseball during my childhood and teen years. I could recognize his voice above all the crowd. Today I watched an old video of my son when he was about four years old. Boy, has his voice changed over the years! God's voice is interesting too. He spoke to Elijah in what was described as a gentle whisper (1 Kings 19:12). Job described His voice as thunder (Job 37:5). David described His voice as powerful enough to break the cedars (Psalm 29:5). One thing is for sure about God's voice: He wants to be heard.

The writer of Hebrews said that in the past God spoke through the prophets and in various ways, but now He speaks through His Son. In other words, if you want to know what God is saying, check out what Jesus said. God will speak to you in a way that will be consistent with His Word. Regardless of how He speaks, with words of warning or words of comfort, we should be thrilled that we matter so much to Him that He wants to communicate something to us.

Respond

The choices we make are largely determined by the voices we listen to. I believe that God loves to speak to us. He loves to communicate to us in such a way that we will listen. Not everyone will respond to a gentle whisper. Some people need to hear the thunder clap of a crisis to hear God speak. Others respond better when they hear a story that relates to them. If we are going to fully discover His purpose for our lives, we must listen to His voice speaking to our heart. Jesus said, "He who has ears; let him hear" (Mark 4:9). What He means is this: "Listen up. I am speaking to you. Pay attention. You need to get this."

Remember

God wants to speak to you today. Will you listen?

God Speaks through His Word

Read
"All Scripture is God-breathed and is useful for teaching, rebuking, correcting and training in righteousness" (2 Timothy 3:16 NIV).

Reflect
"When all else fails, read the directions." How many times have you heard that one? I don't know how many times I have brought something home that needed to be assembled and only read part of the directions to get started. Then I skipped the rest because I thought I was pretty sure of how to finish the job. Almost always, I hit a snag and had to go back and read the rest of the directions. Many times I had to disassemble the mess I had already made in my impatience and then start over. It was always frustrating and made me feel stupid for not following the directions. Who am I to think I can outthink the creator of the product?

This same idea can be applied to the spiritual life. Many times we start out on our Christian journey by reading the Bible consistently, but then after finding out all the good stuff (how to miss hell and hit heaven, etc.), we lay the Bible aside. We say, "I know how to live this Christian life," but before long we hit a snag. And sadly, we don't go back and read the directions. If we did, we would discover some of the great instructions of the Bible.

Respond

You probably have seen or met people who are aimless, having no purpose and no sense of direction. They are being directed by their authority. Whether that authority is their own ability to reason or someone else, their life will never make sense if God's Word is not its authoritative foundation.

The Bible is God's Word to us. Human authors under the supernatural guidance of the Holy Spirit wrote it. It is the supreme source of truth for Christian beliefs and living.

The Bible tells us not only how to be assured of eternal life in heaven but also of how to get the most out of life right now. Isn't it logical that the giver of life would inspire the writing of a book that would teach us how to find meaning in life? God's Word reveals Him. If you want to get to know Him, you must spend time in His Word.

Remember

If your life seems to have hit a snag today, *stop*, go back, and read some of His directions.

God Invites You to Get to Know Him

Read

"Moses said to God, 'Suppose I go to the Israelites and say to them, "The God of your fathers has sent me to you," and they ask me, "What is his name?" Then what shall I tell them'" (Exodus 3:13 NIV)?

Reflect

I don't know Tiger Woods. I know a lot about him through reading, hearing sports reports, and actually watching him play a live practice round of golf, but I don't know *him*. Many people feel the same way about God. They have heard of Him, they have read about Him, and they know people who claim to know Him, but they haven't had the experience of knowing Him. God invites all of us to get to know Him. To some it is in a miraculous way; to others, it is just a simple invitation in a quiet time of their lives. But God extends the invitation to know Him to all.

Moses came to know God through a burning bush experience. When Moses asked God how he should respond if someone asked him about this experience and what he should tell them God's name is, God replied, "Tell them, 'I AM WHO I AM.'" In other words, "I am eternal; I will be what I will be. Whatever you need, that's what I *am*."

During the next forty years, Moses got to know God in an experiential way. He saw Him become the great I AM to all his needs. When he needed to make a difficult decision, God was his Counselor. When he needed courage, God provided it by giving him opportunities to demonstrate courage. When he needed energy, God fueled him with the capacity to move ahead. God has a full supply of everything we need exactly at the time we need it.

Respond

Not everyone has a burning bush experience, but everyone does receive an invitation to know God. His invitation might have come to you as you were reading this devotion. Sometimes He can take a word or phrase and ignite it in your heart to speak to you. He knows how to do that because He knows you. He knows what you need right now. Even more than that, He wants you to experience Him personally. Pursue Him now through prayer. Let Him become your great I Am by trusting Him with your life.

Remember

God has all the supplies you need to become all He desires for you to be.

Taking Giant Steps for God Takes Courage

Read

"Be strong and courageous ... for the Lord your God will be with you wherever you go" (Joshua 1:9 NIV).

Reflect

Years ago an experiment was done to test the power of group pressure. Groups of nine were shown cards with a single line on the left side and three lines on the right side. They were to determine which line on the right was equal in length to the single line on the left. The first eight students had been told ahead of time to select a line that was clearly the wrong one. The test was to determine if the ninth student would select the wrong line as well. The result: almost 40 percent of the subjects participating voted with the majority and made the obvious wrong choice. They lacked the courage to take a stand against the majority.

While the children of Israel were in the wilderness, they didn't have to fight any battles. Oh, they had heard about the battles their forefathers had faced, but they had not experienced any conflict in the wilderness. Soon, however, they were to face the Amorites and the Anakites, who were seasoned in battle and ready to protect their land. The battles belonged to the Lord, but to take this giant step and claim the Promised Land, the Israelites would need a lot of courage. The Anakites were reputed giants. It was even said, "No one could stand up against them" (Deuteronomy 9:2). Therefore, it would have been easy for the Israelites to be intimidated. But the truth was on their side. The Lord had a purpose for them, and part of it was to enter the Promised Land. The Lord had promised them the land, and He would stand with them if they would take a stand for Him.

Respond

One principle that is consistent in Scripture is that God takes a stand for those who stand with Him. The Old Testament records people like Daniel, Shadrach, Meshach, and Abednego, discussing how they courageously took a stand and how God miraculously delivered them from peril. They did not know if God would deliver them or not, but regardless of how God would respond they were determined that it would never be said that they did not take a stand for Him.

Remember

When you stand for God, you will never stand alone.

Ending Before You Begin

Read

"There is a time for everything, and a season for every activity under heaven: a time to be born and a time to die" (Ecclesiastes 3:1–2a NIV).

Reflect

Ending something doesn't get the positive press that starting something does. When you start something, there is excitement, anticipation, and joy. But when you end something, it is often accompanied by feelings of failure or despair. In spite of this reality, the Bible records several positive endings. Take the end of Goliath as an example. The first words David spoke when he heard the giant hurling insults were, "What will be done for the man who kills this Philistine and removes this disgrace from Israel? Who is this uncircumcised Philistine that he should defy the armies of the loving God" (1 Samuel 17:26)? What led to this ending? A passion. A passion to honor God.

Another great ending in the Bible is found in the book of Jonah. Jonah ended his running. His dramatic circumstances led to his repentance. Had he not stopped running, a city would most likely have been destroyed. What led to this ending? A pain. The pain of displeasing God.

Still another great ending came when Paul ended his persecution of Christians (Acts 9). Had he not stopped killing Christians, churches in Philippi, Corinth, Ephesus, and Galatia may never have totally abandoned a works theology for a grace theology. What led to this ending? A person. Paul met Jesus in the most authentic way.

The most redemptive biblical ending occurred when Jesus said, "It is finished," on the cross. He ended the need for a sacrifice for sin. He paid the penalty for all of us. No more sacrifices are needed or required for sin. No more innocent blood needs to be shed. Sin lost. We win, because He ended it. What led to this ending? A promise.

Respond

What needs to end in your life? Does a giant that is intimidating you need to be defeated? Do you need to stop running from God's plan for your life? Do you need to end a damaging attitude toward someone? What will lead to that ending? The answer: a personal relationship with the One who will be there in the end.

Remember

Some things may need to end in your life in order for you to discover the purpose God has for you.

God's Delivery Service, Always Available

Read

"Moses answered the people, 'Do not be afraid. Stand firm and you will see the deliverance the Lord will bring you today. The Egyptians you see today you will never see again'" (Exodus 14:13 NIV).

Reflect

I'm reminded of the story of the man who lost control of his semi as it was going down a mountain. The truck ended up going over the side of the mountain, and the driver was thrown out. As he was flying through the air to his ultimate death, he miraculously caught a branch. Holding on for dear life, he watched his truck explode at the bottom of the mountain. In despair he cried out, "Is there anybody there?" To his surprise, the voice of God answered, saying, "I'm here, and I'll help you." The truck driver replied, "Great, come and help me." God said, "Okay, here's what I want you to do. First, let go of the branch." The truck driver replied, "Is there anybody else there?"

God has been in the rescue business for a long time. He delivered the children of Israel out of Egyptian slavery. The Israelites never saw the Egyptian army again after they took that step of faith and crossed through the Red Sea. He can deliver at anytime, anywhere, and in any way He desires. He has ultimate power to deliver His children. Not only is He capable of delivering us, but also He wants to, if we will let Him. It's important for us to remember who we are in God's eyes. We are those He desires to deliver from the slavery of sin, the wilderness of despair, and the power of evil and worldly forces.

Respond

The real question today is, are you willing to allow God to deliver you from the things that are holding you so tight? Many things can bind us and keep us from being all God desires for us to be. Are you willing to release those things and allow Him to rescue you? Give God some time right now to praise and thank Him for His power to deliver. Confess the times you have been unwilling to let Him take control of your life. Finally, pray that God would strengthen and help you avoid being trapped by the snares of this world.

Remember

God is in the delivery business.

Obedience to His Vision

Read

"Then I heard the voice of the Lord saying, 'Whom shall I send? And who will go for us?' And I said, 'Here I am. Send me!' He said, 'Go and tell this people....' Then I said, 'For how long, O Lord?' And He answered, 'Until the cities lie ruined, and without inhabitant'" (Isaiah 6:8–11 NIV).

Reflect

All of us have in mind what we would like our lives to look like in the future. We have an image of where we would like to be socially, financially, career-wise, and position-wise. These goals are admirable and can be motivating. The great thing is not that you have plans for your life but that God has a plan for your life. He has a vision, a clear mental image, of how He wants your life to look in the future. A vision can be inspiring or intimidating depending on your ability to accept it. Isaiah had just experienced a pretty dramatic worship experience when the Lord asked him a question: "Whom shall I send? And who will go for us?" Because of the vision he had seen, Isaiah responded with a willing heart. Then the Lord gave the assignment. "Go and tell this people." God told Isaiah to go and tell the people what he had experienced with the Lord, but He cautioned him to realize that no one would listen. That is why Isaiah asked, "How long do I have to do this?" The Lord's reply was, basically, "Until there is no one else to tell."

Isaiah, like anyone else, wanted to see some results for his efforts for the Lord. But God said that the most important thing was not to see results but to obey Him. When we obey God, He knows we truly love Him (John 14:15). Our greatest joy should be obedience to God.

Respond
Accepting God's vision for your life depends on how soft your heart is toward Him. To soften your heart, you must view God as a loving Father who has a plan to maximize your giftedness for His kingdom work. That does not mean He has a position or status in mind for you. It means He has plan for you to follow. Are you in tune with that plan?

Remember
You can find meaning for your life by following His plan.

Caution: God at Work

Read

"Continue to work out your salvation with fear and trembling, for it is God who works in you to will and to act according to his good purpose" (Philippians 2:12b–13 NIV).

Reflect

The first time I saw one of those "Have patience, God isn't finished with me yet" bumper stickers, it was on a beat-up old Plymouth, double-parked on a one-way street. I remember thinking, *I wonder if God is going to work on your parking habits next.* The truth is, God is always at work in our lives. We may not notice, we may choose to ignore it, but He is at work around us. In fact, He is trying to help you fulfill the purpose for which He created you. He had a purpose for your life before you were even born. Tragically, many search for that purpose all their lives without consulting or seeking God.

God's purpose for you is to be like Him and to be a reflection of Him on earth. You accomplish that through the various opportunities He gives you daily. Paul said to work out your salvation. That means God has already done a work in you through Jesus to produce love and righteousness. God has gifted you to do His work, but if you neglect that gift or refuse to be obedient, your life will be dormant and joyless.

Respond

What are you working out that people can see? When you know and understand your purpose, you experience joy when you do it. If you refuse to fulfill your purpose in life, you will be frustrated. God made you with a plan in mind. Jeremiah 29:11 reminds us that His plans are to prosper us (we only prosper in God's eyes when we are doing His will), not to harm us (the world system harms us when we buy into what it says is important and we neglect God's plan), and to give us hope and a future (the world system's strategy is to get us to focus only on today and on ourselves, but God's plans for us is to have eternity in mind). His plans for you are eternal. The world's plans for you are temporary. The world will shortchange you. God's plans will reward you forever.

Remember

Be patient. God isn't finished with you yet.

Arrows in Your Quiver

Read

"Like arrows in the hands of a warrior are children born in one's youth. Blessed is the man whose quiver is full of them. They will not be put to shame when they contend with their opponents in court" (Psalm 127:4–5 NIV).

Reflect

J. R. R. Tolkien's *The Lord of the Rings* trilogy depicts the battle between good and evil in addition to the journey of the nine members of the fellowship to destroy the ring. The fight to save Middle Earth is packed with adventure and psychological thrills.

My favorite character is Legolas. The elf archer is an expert marksman, making him a valuable member of the fellowship. His quiet demeanor contrasts sharply with his warrior-like skill with the bow and arrow. Every arrow that he shoots in rapid fire hits its intended target. Seeing his flawless and uninterrupted shooting motion is like watching a graceful ballet dancer. Legolas is always prepared for battle, and the fellowship is glad he is on their side.

The psalmist described children as "arrows in the hands of a warrior." The writer goes on to say, "They will not be put to shame when they contend with their opponents in court." In our world, the Enemy's mind-set is all around us. Our children are headed into battle and they must be prepared.

Many parents do not realize the significance of their mission. They tend to look at children as merely mini look-alikes that will bring them joy and take care of them when they are old. This misconception of parenting could be the downfall of our culture. Arrows are designed to penetrate. If we sharpen our children to the things of God while we have their ear, they could go on to change the world. But if we let the present culture take our place, we will raise a generation of people addicted to the world system and unprepared for battle. The result will be their defeat, their pain, and the proliferation of self-indulgence in our culture.

Respond

Children are a blessing from God entrusted to us to transform the culture. When we help them develop skills to stand for Christ and recognize the pitfalls of the world system, they become arrows in the hands of God to bring about a changed society, thereby enlarging the kingdom of God.

Remember

Children are not only a gift from God. They are our messengers to the future.

An Appetite for His Word

Read
"Like newborn babes, long for the pure milk of the word, so that by it you may grow in respect to salvation" (1 Peter 2:2 NASB).

Reflect
My kids love to read. They got that from their mom. She will read a book from cover to cover no matter how bad it is. She is amazing. One time when she was reading a book, I asked, "How do you like it?" She said, "I hate it. It is so repetitive and so discouraging." I said, "Stop reading it!" She said, "No, I have to finish it—and then I will burn it! I don't want anyone else to have to endure this excruciating and depressing book."

God's Word is just the opposite. It is filled with wisdom, adventure, hope, instruction, and love. Through His Word we can gain meaning for our lives. It is alive in that it leads us to understand and follow God's path to living. When God's Spirit connects our heart to His Word, great change can take place and wonderful things can happen.

Babies have appetites just like all of us. In the same way, when we are born into the family of God, we develop an appetite for His Word. His Word not only gives life and hope but also nourishes us as Christians. His Word is a tremendous guide and encourager as we face the daily challenges of life.

There is a tragedy that exists today within Christian circles, one that weakens our testimony. The tragedy? We often substitute Christian entertainment for getting into His Word.

Sometimes babies do not have an appetite because they have been eating the wrong things—things that may be tasty but not nutritional. The same is true when we try to put other things in place of God's Word.

Respond

A steady diet of God's Word is imperative if we are to mature as healthy Christians. His Word contains milk for spiritual babies to understand who He is. It provides meat for those who are more mature and need to understand their purpose in life. It provides dessert for all of us to enjoy as we read how God worked in the lives of those who came before us.

Remember

Make a habit of coming to His table every day and feeding on His Word.

Relationships

There is nothing more important in this life
or in the next than relationships.

"Let me give you a new command: Love one another. In the
same way I loved you, you love one another. This is how
everyone will recognize that you are my disciples—when they
see the love you have for each other" (John 13:34–35 MSG).

39C

Read

"There is a friend that sticks closer than a brother" (Proverbs 18:24b NIV).

Reflect

My wife, Rhonda, and I were boarding an overseas flight from Europe to the United States when we realized something really terrible. The plane was operating fine. We saw the pilots, and they looked competent enough. So what was the problem? Our seats. I was assigned to 39C, an aisle seat. Rhonda was assigned to 39F, another aisle seat, with one seat in between us. As we looked at the gap between us, we wondered who would show up to take that seat. I already didn't like that person. We sat and waited, both of us praying that nobody would show up. We kept our heads facing down and our prayers going up, asking God to show us favor and mercy and let this seat in between us remain empty.

I realize there is trouble in the Middle East. I also know that thousands of people are out of work. In other words, I knew God had a full plate, but all I could do was look at that empty seat next to me and pray that God would keep it that way for the next nine hours. Funny, isn't it? We don't deny there are problems going on around us, but whenever our closeness to the one we love is threatened, nothing else matters.

Guess what? No one showed up. Even though God's plate was full, His heart was fuller. His love showered down on a guy who was selfish and said, "Here's your empty seat. Stretch out and enjoy the one you love."

Respond
Have you ever felt there was a gap between you and the one you love? Distance has a way of disconnecting people unless you are intentional about closing the gap. God has been intentional about closing the gap between you and Him, so much so that He sent His Son to bridge the gap so you can connect to Him. The cost was high and the journey was long, but He made the trip, paid the price, and set down in your world. He offers you a seat with Him in heaven if you will just receive His free gift of forgiveness and salvation.

Remember
God wants to close the distance between Him and you.

A Love Relationship Like No Other

Read

"Love the Lord your God with all your heart and with all your soul and with all your mind and with all your strength" (Mark 12:30 NIV).

Reflect

For years, my wife has prayed the above Scripture for me. She figured if I loved the Lord with all my heart, soul, mind, and strength, I'd be a pretty good husband and father. Pretty good plan, isn't it?

Jesus called this the greatest of all the commandments. If you can get a handle on this commandment and let it dominate your attitude and actions, then the other commandments will be much easier for you to follow. When you love God with all that is within you (your mind, will, and emotions), you can better avoid all the "do not" commandments of Christianity that destroy your character if you engage in them, like lying, stealing, killing, etc. He made it simpler for us. He narrowed the Ten Commandments down to two—love God and love people.

Living a life of love is strange to the world. The media equates love with sex and will sometimes portray love simply as admiration. But these by-products of love are not love. Love is a decision and a commitment entered into by the person who chooses to love. God chose to love you. He looked down and saw you with all your faults and chose to love you. There is nothing you can do that will stop that choice. He loves you, period.

Respond

The question is, do you love God? Have you chosen to love Him, or have you chosen to take advantage of His love? Do you continue your sinful habits and count on Him to love you and forgive you even though you willingly disobey Him? If you do, you're taking advantage of His love. But if you're following His desires, you've been changed by His love. And there is no other love relationship like that.

In John 15:12, Jesus said we are to love as He has loved us. So, how has he loved us? He has forgiven us. Do you have someone you need to forgive? He has blessed us. Is there someone who needs the blessing of your attention and resources today? He has accepted us. Anyone longing for your acceptance today? We are not just to love. We are to love *as He loved us*.

Remember

Love is a choice—the best choice.

A Relationship That Can Simplify Your Life

Read

"The most important is ... And you shall love the Lord your God. ... The second is this, You shall love your neighbor as yourself. There is no other commandment greater than these" (Mark 12:29–31 ESV).

Reflect

Early in my ministry I interviewed for a ministerial position at a church. I asked the interviewer what the church was looking for in a person to fill the position. He said, "We want someone who will love God and love people." Thinking he did not understand my question, I decided to rephrase it in order to find out the details of the job description. So I said, "Okay, but what do you want this person to do?" He replied, "We want him to love God and love people." I thought maybe I was not being specific enough, so I countered with, "Okay, so let's say I come into the office on Monday morning. What do I do?" He said, "You will love God and love people." I said, "Okay, let me see if I've got this straight. You want someone to come to your church and love God and love people?" He said, "You've got it!" That's a pretty simple message, isn't it?

During Jesus' ministry when He was asked, "What is the greatest of all the commandments?", He said to love the Lord your God with all your heart, soul, mind, and strength (i.e., to love God), and to love your neighbor as yourself (i.e., to love people). He simplified it.

Respond

Are you trying to make life too complicated? Do you think if you do this or that, it will make you a good person? Step back for a minute. Don't let it take so long for you to get it. Let Jesus's words simplify it for you. Love God and love people. Do this and you fulfill all the law. But first you must have a relationship with God. You must love Him. How much? Enough to give Him your life. Have you done that? Spend some time with Him in prayer right now. If you haven't given Him your life, do it today. Ask Him to forgive you of your sins and to take control of your life. Let Him simplify your life today.

Remember

Love God and love people today.

A Strong Marriage Is a Big Deal to God

Read

"This is another thing you do. You cover the Lord's altar with your tears. You cry and moan, because he does not accept your offerings and is not pleased with what you bring. You ask, 'Why?' It is because the Lord sees how you treated the wife you married when you were young. You broke your promise to her, even though she was your partner and you had an agreement with her" (Malachi 2:13–14 NCV).

Reflect

It was a night to remember, the night when I went into my future father-in-law's office and asked him for his only daughter's hand in marriage. When I told him that I loved his daughter very much and would like to ask him for her hand in marriage, you could have heard a pin drop. The silence seemed eternal as he paused and thought through his response. My heartbeat accelerated as I wondered what he would say. Finally, he asked, "Thomas [using my formal name was an indication of seriousness], what if I say no?" In all my preparation for this moment, I never expected this response. However, thinking back, I see that it was a good question. With a lump in my throat, I replied, "Well, Sir, I would respect that, because I respect you. But that wouldn't change anything." As those words passed my lips, I remember thinking, *Was that too bold? Was it disrespectful? Was it rude?* Quite the contrary; it was just what he wanted to hear. He wanted to hear that I was totally committed to his daughter and that nothing would change that fact.

In the same way, God takes marriage very seriously. He is not impressed with how much we serve Him if we are breaking our promise to our mate. He demands that we keep our commitment to our mate. If we don't, He will not be pleased.

Respond

Here are some tips that will help you treat your mate better this week: (1) Take time in the evening to just listen to your spouse. Give your mate all the time he or she needs to share feelings about his or her day. (2) Do something for your spouse. Perform an act of service that he or she would appreciate. (3) Tell your loved one *why* you love him or her. Give some reasons why you're so glad your spouse married you. (4) Show some affection.

Remember

Keep your vows.

Coming to Your Senses

Read

"When he came to his senses" (Luke 15:17 NIV).

Reflect

I will never forget what one loving mother wrote on her teenage daughter's medical form before she sent her on a ski trip to Colorado. The form covered typical vaccinations as well as information about allergies and medications. One blank on the form asked for any other health-related information that the leaders of the trip might need to know about the student. This mother wrote the following line: "She has occasional fits of stupidity." We all do, don't we? There are times when all of us get outside our senses. We all experience times when we aren't thinking right. We believe lies or else we launch off into some selfish venture that blinds us from believing that anything hurtful could happen to us.

The rebellious son of Luke 15 was living a life that didn't make any sense. Considering his background, the privileges he had experienced, and the resources available to him at home, his riotous lifestyle was a "fit of stupidity." However, it was the pain of that senseless lifestyle that helped him remember something that made all the sense in the world: a life with his father. He remembered his father's wealth, how well his hired hands were cared for, and the fact that they lived productive lives. He considered the insanity of starving to death. As he reflected on his situation, he came to the conclusion that his desperation must trump his pride.

Respond

The son's rehearsal of his speech indicates that he thought he needed to prepare an articulate appeal to his father's common-sense way of thinking. He may have thought that since his father didn't chase after him, he would expect an apology as well as a method of being paid back for the loss of work the son could have produced on the farm. Was he in for a surprise! The father disregarded the speech. The son never had a chance to finish it. All the father wanted was for the son to return home. He was more interested in his heart's being found than his work's being lost.

Remember

If you have taken a prodigal detour, returning to the Father makes all the sense in the world.

Compliments

Read

"Let everything you say be good and helpful, so that your words will be an encouragement to those who hear them" (Ephesians 4:29 NIV).

Reflect

We can't ever really get enough of these things. No, they are not made of chocolate, but they do come in all shapes and sizes. They're actually sweeter than chocolate. Even more surprising, they're healthy, good for your heart. We don't have to have them, but we all want them. The truth is we all need them. In fact, we crave them. They never leave us feeling empty. They always fill us, but we seem always to have room for more. Kids love them. They will do almost anything to get them. People can, and often do, live without them, but it is sad to see—and the result is a miserable existence. What are these people missing? What is this sweet nectar that strengthens, and always brings life and a smile to every face? Compliments, the sweet words of affirmation that say, "You are really good." Do you remember the last one you received? I bet you do. If you don't, it's been too long.

Respond

For many of us, compliments are much easier to receive than to give. We hold them in, because either we don't know how to deliver them or we think they will not be well received. Jesus gave a lot of compliments. He not only gave them liberally, but

He also placed them strategically. In fact, in the last book in the Bible He spoke to seven churches and began six of those conversations with a compliment. His compliments set the stage for lifesaving correction. How sad that many of us today spill out words of correction like pouring milk over cereal but that we hold in words of affirmation as if in a welded vault. We wonder why our words of correction are not well received. Perhaps it's because they need to be preceded and softened with compliments that encourage.

Words will go a long way. For some they will last a lifetime. Your kids or spouse can live off your compliments for days, weeks, and months—sometimes even years. When people believe and internalize praises, those words can become a part of their character, determining how hard they try and who they become.

Remember
If you sincerely compliment someone today, you gain a friend for tomorrow.

Do You Love Me?

Read

"When they had finished eating, Jesus said to Simon Peter, 'Simon son of John, do you truly love me more than these'" (John 21:15 NIV)?

Reflect

When you were a kid in second or third grade and you had a crush on someone, did you ever pick up a daisy, pull its petals off, and say, "He loves me. He loves me not" (or, "She loves me. She loves me not")?

At the end of Jesus's time on earth, He had an encounter with Peter when He was testing Peter's love level. They had been through a lot together, but now Jesus was about to leave earth and He wanted to know where Peter stood. Interesting. Jesus wants to know where we all stand when it comes to Him. Jesus had seen Peter at his best and at his worst. Jesus had stood on the platform as Peter rode the roller coaster of life, experiencing the highs and lows of the Christian life. And now, just before Jesus was to make His ascension to heaven, He wanted to know how much Peter loved Him.

Why does Jesus need to hear Peter say that he loves Him? Because Jesus had plans for Peter, and the success of those plans would hinge on the depth of Peter's love. Now, Peter had just come off of some pretty weak moments. In earlier chapters we see how he denied even knowing Jesus—not once, but three times within just a few hours. When the pressure came, he folded. So now, Jesus asks, "Do you love me?" Not once, but three times. Perhaps one for every denial? Maybe. We don't know for sure, but we do know the question was important, as was the answer.

Respond

Grace often comes in the form of second and third chances. We don't deserve those extended opportunities, but they are simply given to us by mates, parents, and even bosses. But they are often rare. When second chances are given, they usually come with strings attached. "I will give you another chance, but ..." However, such is not the case with Jesus. His second chances are unconditional, undeserved, unwavering, and unbelievable! It's called grace. And it comes with *no strings attached*.

Remember

Grace is yours for the receiving but also for the distributing.

Farsighted

Read

"But while he was still a long way off, his father saw him" (Luke 15:20 NIV).

Reflect

My dad was the first person I knew who was farsighted. He could clearly see things a good distance away. I remember as a child being amazed at how well he could spot a small animal standing five hundred meters away in a field, or the stars of the Little Dipper in the night sky. Being nearsighted myself, I was always impressed by his ability to spot things before I could.

As I grew older, I discovered that most loving fathers are farsighted, not farsighted with their eyesight but with their perspective. Loving fathers realize that life is a journey, not an event. When a child messes up, rebels, or embarrasses the family name, the loving father looks past the negative event and searches for a far greater purpose that God is orchestrating. It doesn't mean he isn't disappointed with his child's behavior. It doesn't mean he isn't hurt. But the farsighted father always has hope in God to change the heart of a selfish child.

The loving father who had two prodigal sons in Luke 15 was farsighted. It's easy to imagine that every day his eyes were searching the horizon for the silhouette of his wayward son. He knew his walk and could recognize his unique gait from a distance. When his son appeared "still a long way off," this farsighted father did something rarely done by older Jewish men. He ran. Jesus's story of the prodigal son describes to us what our heavenly Father is like. He is farsighted, looking for our return, ready to run to our side in order to stop our repentant speech and start the party. That's what God is like.

Respond

Is God looking for you to return to Him? Remember: He can see you. His relationship with you is constantly on His mind. He recognizes your heart. He looks past the events of today and scans the horizon of the future, looking for your return. When you seek Him, you will find Him searching, looking for you with a loving heart and open arms.

Remember

If you have walked away from your heavenly Father, you can always return, no questions asked.

Fellowship with Meaning

Read

"They devoted themselves to the apostles' teaching and to the fellowship, to the breaking of bread and to prayer" (Acts 2:42 NIV).

Reflect

Here is one of my favorite little poems:

> To live above with those we love, O that will be glory.
> To live below with those we know, well, that's another story.

Isn't that funny! We all know people who get on our nerves—those people you enjoy being around for maybe two minutes. Now, getting along with God may not be a problem for you, but getting along with some other believers may be tough. Why? Here's my theory: The closer you get to God, the more divine you see He is. The closer you get to others, the more human you see they are. But the honest truth is this: even when people can be jerks, we still need each other and we need to have fellowship with other people. God made us to be social beings. Through that social contact we learn better how to relate to Him. Jesus said, "A new command I give you: Love one another. As I have loved you, so you must love one another. By this everyone will know that you are my disciples, if you love one another" (John 13:24–35).

Fellowship is defined as "having in common." It also means, "to share." True fellowship fills a person's inner need for love and acceptance. The world today is filled with people who look contented, but on the inside they are crying out for someone to show them that they care. We all need love. When we demonstrate love, those around us will become more open to fellowship. Love opens the door to strengthening relationships. Have you opened that door in someone's life recently?

Respond
Besides filling the need for love and acceptance, fellowship also fills the need to be heard and encouraged. It meets the need to feel supported and be reproved when necessary. True fellowship calls you out when you get off track and loves you through difficult times. When Christians are demonstrating healthy fellowship, people are drawn to it. Have you found the fellowship you need to help you grow as an authentic Christian? Your growth as a believer depends largely on the people with whom you choose to fellowship.

Remember
The key of love opens the door of fellowship.

Forgive and Be Forgiven

Read

"Then the master called the servant in. 'You wicked servant,' he said. 'I canceled all that debt of yours because you begged me to. Shouldn't you have had mercy on your fellow servant just a I had on you'" (Matthew 18:32–33 NIV)?

Reflect

Whenever you are wronged, forgiveness is not a natural response. When we are robbed of something, we naturally want the one who robbed us to feel the same as we do—or a little worse. We want retribution. We want someone to hurt like we hurt—or a little worse. The idea of forgiveness is completely foreign to us the moment we are hurt. However, for the believer, forgiveness is to be our supernatural response. We cannot do it on our own. We need an example to help us. We need strength from outside ourselves to embolden us not to seek revenge but to seek rest. For if we do not forgive, we will be inviting bitterness and unrest in our lives, which can ultimately destroy us.

Jesus told the story in Matthew 18:32–35 in order to show how much God has forgiven us. The man in question owed an amount he was incapable of repaying. His situation was hopeless. The compassion of his master was his only chance. His master graciously forgave (canceled) the debt. But then the man went and found someone who owed him a small, insignificant amount of money ($1; the average daily wage was one penny). When the second man asked for patience like the first man had with his creditor, the first man, who had been forgiven so much, had the second man thrown in prison. Perhaps he had the legal right to do so, but he did not have the moral right.

Respond

May I ask you a personal question? Who hurt you? Has the pain of that person's offense drifted into other areas of your life? Do you find yourself wanting to hurt others as a result of the hurt your feel? Or, instead of hurting others, do you want to build walls and not let anyone into your life? Either way, you lose. To learn forgiveness is to learn the way of God. For no one forgives better. Learn to forgive today.

Remember

Forgiveness is God's supernatural response to those who have wronged Him.

Good Friends Are Hard to Find

Read
"For Demas, having loved this present world has deserted me" (2 Timothy 4:10 NASB).

Reflect
What words would you use to describe your closest friends? My closest friends are unassuming, totally accepting, and fun. Their level of love is unquestionable, and their level of availability is unmatched. They will be there when I need them, and their entire motivation will be just to help. They truly add value to my life. I am not the person I am without them. The bottom line is they care. Not only do they care about me, but they also care about what I care about. They love what I love even if it is not their thing. They show interest because they are interested in me. Everyone needs friends like this.

However, good friends sometimes are hard to find. Paul had a close friend named Demas who worked with him. Demas knew the kind of guy Paul was and even stayed with him during his last term in prison. Yet, at the most inopportune time, Demas left Paul. No, he didn't just leave Paul; he deserted Paul. He deserted Paul, not because of fear, but because he loved the world system. When the going got tough, Demas said, "I don't need this. I'm going to live it up. I can't take the pressure anymore." What a disappointment for Paul, to spend time developing someone and then, when the hard times come, that person left him alone.

Do you see what the world can do to Christian brothers? It can literally make us desert one another.

Respond

What kind of friend are you? The key to having good friends is to be a good friend. Good friends do not take the easy way out. They do not desert you when you are down. When you have someone who sticks with you in difficult times, you have truly found a friend.

For what price would you desert a friend? Are you the type of friend who sticks no matter the pressure? If you are, you're in good company. Jesus is that type of friend to all who follow Him.

Remember

"A friend loves at all times, and a brother is born for adversity" (Proverbs 17:17 NASB).

Grandparents Love Fiercely

Read

"A good person leaves an inheritance for their children's children" (Proverbs 13:22 NIV).

Reflect

I assume you have heard all the lines "There is nothing like being a grandparent. You are going to love it! You can spoil them and then send them home. I wish I could have been a grandparent first." I remembered thinking that new grandparents were a little crazy. I felt like saying to them, "Hey, I'll be the judge of what I am going to love and how much I will like being a grandparent." Today, I'm a grandparent and I'm here to say, "There is nothing like it in the world." I totally underestimated how much fun this experience would be. I have become a child again. My love level has been transformed by new life.

The writer of Proverbs says that a good person leaves an inheritance for his or her grandchildren. This means that grandparents are to value their grandchildren by giving them something that will last beyond the grandparent's life. That inheritance need not be limited to money. The money will be gone and forgotten, but the wise grandparent leaves more than money. Wise grandparents can leave an inheritance of unconditional love and lasting character-building memories. They can leave stories and values that have come from a life fully lived. They can leave a practical model of loving and giving.

Grandparents have the unique opportunity to touch a day they will never see through their grandchildren.

Respond
My father-in-law treated our kids like a treasure. His grandchildren were the apple of his eye. He never demeaned them or made fun of them. He loved them fiercely by wrestling them, playing with them, and always respecting them. Some would say he spoiled them. But his love for them was more than that. He connected with them by the way he respected and valued them. Watching him made me a better parent and a better grandparent. I learned to love in three ways: intentionally, respectfully, and prayerfully. A grandparent has a special voice in the heart of a child. They have an understanding to share that a parent sometimes has difficulty finding because of the demands of parenting. As parents have to provide the law and discipline, grandparents can supply the love and grace.

Remember
You can touch a day you will never see through the next generation. How are you treating them?

.

Influencing Others by Confronting Them

Read

"This man was handed over to you by God's set purpose and foreknowledge; and you, with the help of wicked men, put him to death by nailing him to the cross" (Acts 2:23 NIV).

Reflect

If you enjoy confrontation, there is probably something wrong with you. I mean, if you really look forward to letting people have it, then you need to calm down. Normally, people do not enjoy confrontation. Yet, just as the Bible says, there is a time for everything, meaning that there is a time to confront. One reason we do not like confrontation is that often we are afraid of rejection. However, when confrontation is presented with the other party's best interests in mind and in a spirit of love, it can be effective and productive. Later in Acts 2, Luke recorded, "When the people heard this, they were cut to the heart and said to Peter and the other apostles, 'Brothers what shall we do?'" It was at that time Peter gave them instructions on how to become Christians. It was not until they were confronted that they responded to the message Peter had delivered.

Some people respond well to confrontation. When the prophet Nathan confronted King David about his adultery, and because David knew in his heart that Nathan was right, David responded positively to Nathan's confrontation. Was it pleasant? Not at all. Was it worth it? Absolutely.

It is important to remember that many times before confrontation occurs, some groundwork needs to be done. Nathan told David an innocent story that introduced the confrontation. Jesus often confronted through the use of parables. Peter's confrontation in Acts 2 was in defense of the behavior of fellow believers at the Jewish celebration of Pentecost. Some sort of groundwork was laid in all these situations.

Respond
Do you need to deal with some things in your life that you have been letting go, thinking you could fix them on your own? Have you confronted yourself in a way that has led to change? Do you need to confront someone in love? Has the groundwork been laid? Remember that effective confrontation is done in love and with the other party's best interests in mind. Ask God for wisdom, and follow His lead.

Remember
When you lay the proper groundwork, confrontation can have positive results.

Influencing Others by Telling Your Story

Read
"Then, leaving her water jar, the woman went back to the town and said to the people, 'Come, see a man who told me everything I ever did'" (John 4:28–29 NIV).

Reflect
Have you ever had such good news that you thought you would burst if you did not tell someone? Maybe it was an engagement or a newborn baby, but the toughest thing for you to do was to keep it to yourself. This was the way it was with the woman Jesus met at a well in Samaria. She had never met anyone like Him. He basically revealed to her that He knew her and He wanted her to experience a new life.

In spite of the fact that this woman had limited knowledge of spiritual things, she did know that one day a Messiah would come. When she met Him face-to-face, her response was to put her trust and faith in Him. Her immediate response after her conversion was to share her story with someone. Even though she still had limited knowledge, she did have the knowledge of her experience and the zeal to tell it. She didn't know everything there was to know about Jesus, but she knew enough to share with her friends.

You may not know all there is to know about Scripture or all there is to know about God. You may not even know all the disciples or books of the Bible. Fortunately, those things are not required before you can become a Christian. But if you have experienced the forgiveness of your sins through faith in Jesus Christ, you have a story to tell.

Respond

Did you notice that the Bible indicates that the woman, "leaving her water jar," went back to the town and invited people to come meet Jesus? In order to share your faith, sometimes you have to leave your routine. Her impression of Jesus was so powerful that she was compelled to drop everything and tell her story to someone. The result? "Many of the Samaritans from that town believed in him because of the woman's testimony, 'He told me everything I ever did'" (John 4:39).

Remember

Your story of how God has worked in your life is compelling to someone.

Joy and Relief

Read

"And when he finds it, he joyfully puts it on his shoulders and goes home. Then he calls his friends and neighbors together and says, 'Rejoice with me; I have found my lost sheep'" (Luke 15:5–6 NIV).

Reflect

My wife lost her engagement ring. She prayed about it. She told me about it. We prayed. We figured that God knew where it was. He did. We found it a year and a half later. Have you ever lost something that was important to you? If you found it, do you remember how you felt? Relieved? Peaceful? Ecstatic? All these are reasonable and natural responses to recovering something that was lost. Whether it's your keys or a valuable ring that you have misplaced, there is always a sense of joy and relief when you find it.

In Luke 15, Jesus concludes each story by saying there was rejoicing when what was missing was rescued. Rescued. That's a pretty good word to describe what some of our friends need, isn't it? They need to be rescued from what has them bound. It could be an addiction they can't shake or a habit that they refuse to break. Perhaps you have family members who have the same need. They need to be rescued. Just like the rebellious son who left home, or the lost coin, or the sheep that wandered away, they need to be rescued from what might happen to them. But just like the sheep and the son, our friends and family members do not realize the danger they are in. They have been lulled into a desensitized state that prohibits them from recognizing their dangerous situation. They need a wake-up call.

Respond

Maybe today you need to be rescued. Jesus made a request of those who need to be rescued. He simply said, "Come to Me" (Matthew 11:28). When you come to Him you can experience joy and relief.

Perhaps you know of a friend or family member who doesn't know the Lord personally. Wouldn't it be great if somehow that person would come to a place in life where he or she would admit that he or she needs Jesus Christ as Savior and thereafter commit his or her life to Him? To think that the person would be able to spend eternity with you would no doubt be one of your greatest joys.

Remember

His invitation to joy and relief: "Come to Me."

God Is Love

Read
"Dear friends, let us love one another, for love comes from God. Everyone who loves has been born of God and knows God. Whoever does not love does not know God, because God is love" (1 John 4:7–8 NIV).

Reflect
Have you ever been wrong? Rhonda and I were checking into a motel late one night. We had been on the road all day and were really tired. I did what I normally do. I pulled up to the door of the motel, got out of the car, and went inside to see if they had any rooms (I know I should have made reservations). I got the room and then parked the car. She got her things. I got the luggage. In these situations, I never tell her the room number (just a controlling head game I play). I just say, "Come on," and she follows me. We went up the elevator and then walked down the hallway to the room. I slid the key card. Nothing happened. I slid it again. Nothing. She said, "Is this the right room?" "Yes," I said. I slid the card again, and then we heard people talking and scurrying around in the room. Rhonda said, "Tom, this is the wrong room!" At the same time I said, "Someone is in our room!" After all, I couldn't be the person who was wrong. Then I looked at the paper key pouch on which the room number was written. I looked on the door of the room. Wrong room. "One flight down," I said. Have you ever been wrong but felt with all your heart you were right? Feelings can play tricks on you.

Some people are wrong about God and how He loves. In their heart they feel they are right, but they have taken a wrong turn. Their key is not working, and somehow they have arrived at the wrong place. And because they do not understand His love, they have trouble loving others.

Respond
Here is what God's Word teaches about His love. His love *accepts* you completely. Do you know what acceptance means? It means that He will love you no matter what. It means that you do not have to do anything for Him to love you. It means that His love for you is not based on your performance.

Remember
God loves you no matter what! (Oh, and check your key-card pouch!)

Love in Action

Read

"This is love for God: to obey his commands. And His commands are not burdensome" (1 John 5:3 NIV).

Reflect

I'll never forget the night my wife, Rhonda, and I left the church we had served for years to go to Kansas City to further my education. The night we left, the church threw a big party in our honor (which we didn't deserve). We found all the gifts given—and nice words said—very humbling and unmerited. At the close of the evening, we were given a going-away present, a check for $1,000. We were blown away (that was a lot of money in 1981!). I will never forget the memo line on that check. It read, "Love in Action." From that moment on, I have measured my own love not by what I say, but by what I do to demonstrate it.

How do you know when people love you? Do you know it because they tell you? Some would say yes, but others would say, "Just telling me isn't enough; you need to show me." God says if we love Him, we will show it. We will show it by our obedience. But it's much more than just our obedience. Notice the last part of today's verse: "His commands are not burdensome." You see, those who really love God do not obey Him out of fear but out of love. They obey Him because they want to. It's a joy to go His way because they trust Him.

Respond

Your love for God is a question of motivation. What motivates you to obey Him? Your love? Why do you serve Him? Because of your deep love and devotion to the One who gave His life for you, or because of the image you want people to see? These are searching questions, but they are valid.

God's relationship with you is based on His love for you. He loves you so much that He made you in His image. He paid the penalty for your sin, and He provides His Spirit to live in you to help you have a meaningful life.

Spend some time with God now and ask Him to search your heart and motives. Let His Spirit guide you and lead you to a point of assurance giving you the knowledge that your love is pure and true and that your works are genuine and faithful to Him.

Remember

Love is a verb!

Maturing in Relationships

Read

"For you are still fleshly. For since there is jealousy and strife among you, are you not fleshly and are you not walking like mere men" (1 Corinthians 3:3 NASB)?

Reflect

You do not have to be around someone very long to tell where he or she is spiritually. Typically the person's language and behavior give it away. Most of the time you can see rather easily if God's Word is influencing someone. It is not revealed in how much Scripture the person has memorized, even though it is very important to internalize His Word. Although Scripture memorization is admirable, it is not the acid test to prove that someone is maturing spiritually. How can you tell if someone is truly growing spiritually? It is revealed by how he or she treats others. The person's relationships are the chief indicator of whether or not his or her spiritual walk is authentic. The true test to see if those spiritual exercises are connecting to a mature faith will be manifested as the person's love for others.

I know a lot of spiritually maturing people who just do not have the gift of memorizing Scripture, but they are intentional about meeting the needs of others. Their behavior authenticates their faith. On the other hand, I know people who love to study God's Word but who are impatient and critical of others. Within five minutes of a conversation, they are talking bad about someone and gossiping. But those who are maturing have developed a deeper level of patience and understanding with others. They have self-control and are wired to help, not to harm. Their maturity is revealed in their relationships.

Respond

Bible study is important. Prayer is a must. Hanging out with believers to receive encouragement and support cannot be undersold when it comes to living the Christian life. But unless your Bible study, prayer, and fellowship lead to serving others and being a blessing to those in need, you are missing what following Christ is all about. Jesus did not say you would recognize His true followers by how many Bible studies they attend. He said the thing that will give us away, the thing you will notice more than anything else, is our love for one another.

Remember

"By this everyone will know that you are my disciples, if you love one another" (John 13:35 NIV).

Motivated by His Love

Read

"We love because He first loved us" (1 John 4:19 NIV).

Reflect

God is love. The Bible is clear on this point. You need not question His love, because it can be found in the Scriptures from cover to cover. In the Old Testament, the law was "before the eyes" of God's people, but they still sinned. Today the laws of the land are before our eyes, and we still break them. If we have trouble obeying the rules of life, it could be that our eyes are focused on the wrong thing.

The best motivation for obeying God is not His laws but His *love*. For example, when Peter denied Christ, saying he didn't know Him, his sorrow was not because he broke a law. He felt bad because he hurt the One he loved and the One who loved him. Peter loved Jesus because he first had experienced love from Him. He knew in all his weaknesses and sin that Jesus really loved him and cared about him. The same is true for you.

The psalmist put it this way: "For your love is ever before me, and I walk continually in your truth" (Psalm 26:3). When your eyes are on God and His love, you are motivated to abstain from evil, to do good, and to walk in truth.

Now answer these questions: Are you practicing sin? Are there sinful patterns in your life right now that are robbing your joy and disappointing the Savior? If so, then God's love is probably not "ever before you" and you are not being motivated by His love. Look to the One who loves you the most and stop sinning. His love is the ultimate motivator.

Respond

Have you ever been burned by fake love? Perhaps someone told you that he or she loved you and then later you saw that this person's behavioral patterns were not consistent with his or her proclamation of love for you. Few things are more hurtful than to have someone tell you that he or she loves you only for you to see his or her actions betray those words.

All love originates with God. He is the love Creator. He knows what authentic love is because He is the Source of it. For us to experience authentic love, we must get to know Him personally.

Remember

Keep God's love ever before you and you will be motivated to share His love.

Open Your Eyes

Read

"Do you not say, 'Four months more and then the harvest?' I tell you, open your eyes and look at the fields! They are ripe for harvest" (John 4:35 NIV).

Reflect

Everyone has needs. We have physical needs, emotional needs, social needs, financial needs, and spiritual needs just to name a few. However, oftentimes it is difficult to notice some of these needs in others. People wear masks, hide their emotions, and camouflage their needs. Many of us want others to think we are normal. What we fail to realize is that needy is normal. No matter what your status, no matter how much money you have, you have needs.

When the disciples returned from town with food, they found Jesus talking to a Samaritan woman at the community well. They waited until He was finished and then offered Him food. Jesus told them that His "food" was to do the will of the Father. Then He said what is recorded in today's verse. Jesus didn't say this to be disrespectful to those who had brought Him food; instead, He said it to show them the urgency of doing God's will by sharing the gospel. While they were gone, He had been visiting with a needy woman. The conversation changed her life. Jesus saw needy people who were ready for life change and offered it to them.

Many of us put off sharing the love of God with others. We think there will be another chance. But Jesus is saying that we need to be sensitive to those around us now, because they are drinking from a well that only temporarily satisfies. We are not to have the mind-set that the harvest is a long way off; instead, we should see that today may be a day we can point someone to Christ. If we wake up every day with that attitude, we will be ready for and sensitive to those around us who need Him.

Respond

Are you sensitive to those in your corner of the world who need Christ? One of the first steps to reaping the harvest is to plant the seed. Just start praying for that person. Then water the seed through your behavior and attitude. God will use you when you are faithful to pray and persist.

Remember

Open your eyes to the needs around you. You can have a part in changing someone's life for eternity.

Preparing for Life Where You Are Going

Read

"My Father's house has many rooms; if that were not so, would I have told you that I am going there to prepare a place for you? And if I go and prepare a place for you, I will come back and take you to be with me that you also may be where I am" (John 14:2–3 NIV).

Reflect

I recently read this entry in my journal from a few years ago:

> I just got on a plane headed from Fort Lauderdale to St. Louis. The temperature in Fort Lauderdale is 85 degrees. In St. Louis it is 25 degrees. I see a lot of people in shorts and light clothing getting on the plane. Their clothes are nice. They appear to be very comfortable. They look good, just not prepared for what they are about to experience. PREDICTION: I will hear a lot of complaining from these folks when we get to St. Louis. They will be critics of the weather and not their preparation for it.

Jesus knew that preparation was important. Life will not always be like it is right now. We will not always live on this earth. Things will change for us. We will fly to another destination if we know Him personally. This is a place for which we need to prepare. We prepare for it by clothing ourselves in His righteousness. When you give Him your life, He responds by giving you His Spirit to come to live in you and by promising you a crown of righteousness in the future (2 Timothy 4:8).

So many go through life discouraged and negative. Bad things happen, and they sometimes surprise us. But don't complain. Prepare. Prepare for the cold, the snow, and the ice of life.

Respond

God has a perfect place prepared for those who love Him. First Corinthians 2:9 tells us that no one can imagine what God has prepared for those who love Him. We don't know the climate, but we do know the Christ who prepared it. Since He is perfect, we can be assured that the place He is preparing is perfect too. But you must know Him personally to go there.

The last line of this journal entry read, "I just heard someone say, 'Look, there is snow on the ground down there.' And so it begins."

Remember

He loves you so much that He wants you to live with Him forever.

Real Worship

"Ezra opened the book. ... The people all stood up. Ezra praised the Lord, the great God; and all the people lifted their hands and responded, 'Amen! Amen!' Then they bowed down and worshipped the Lord with their faces to the ground" (Nehemiah 8:5–6 NIV).

Reflect

Have you ever been to a worship service where all the people stood when God's Word was read? This Scripture is the basis of that demonstration of worship. When Ezra read God's Word, the people showed respect by standing, and they stood for hours listening to His Word. They listened intently with the expectation that they were about to hear from God Almighty. This is the attitude and mind-set we are to have as we open God's Word.

Worship takes place when God is honored. When Ezra opened God's Word, the people knew they would hear the Word of God and not merely the ideas of a mortal man. Isn't it interesting how they treated God's Word differently than they would have done had it merely been a man's words they were about to hear? These people were hungry for a Word from God and were willing to block out half a day to hear God speak to them. This resulted in worship. Praise broke out and people humbled themselves before God. They were not worshipping the Book that was being read; they were worshipping the God who was speaking through the Book.

Respond

When was the last time you were so hungry for God's Word in your life that you prioritized half a day to spend in His Word, reading, studying, and expecting Him to speak to you? When I have done this exercise, I always, without exception, come back home loving my wife more and being committed more than ever to being a better, more caring husband. I am more sensitive to my children, and it seems like I enjoy them more than ever after I've spent an extended period of time with God. It helps me better understand the Scripture in Jeremiah 29:13, when God said, "You will ... find me when you seek me with all your heart." If you are willing to block out the time and seek Him, He will reveal Himself to you, whether it is by reading the Bible, praying, or a still, small voice impressing your conscience.

Remember

He speaks to us through His Word.

Sacrificial Giving

Read
"But even if I am being poured out like a drink offering on the sacrifice and service coming from your faith, I am glad and rejoice with all of you" (Philippians 2:17 NIV).

Reflect
I never look at giving of myself to my wife, my children, or my grandchildren as a sacrifice. Why? Because I love them so much. In fact, when I'm not willing to sacrifice for them, it indicates how much I love me more than I love them. When I do give to them and see how it impacts their lives, I have a joy that could never be achieved by keeping my time and resources to myself.

Paul was willing to pour out his life for the sake of the church and to do it joyfully. He was so in love with the church that he was willing to give everything. This would be considered the ultimate in giving, that is, sacrificing your life for others. The reason for Paul's attitude was that his confidence was not in what he had—his confidence was in Christ. He knew how deep his love for Christ was and that Christ would never forsake him in his sacrificial giving. Therefore, to sacrifice on the behalf of others was a joy for Paul.

Respond
How much have you sacrificed for those you love? Have you consistently been willing to give in order that they may be productive? How about the church? What is your attitude about

sacrificing for God's people? Have you considered using your time and resources to enhance the ministry of the church to others? If the church is to make an impact on the culture, it will take sacrifice, just as Christ sacrificed for us. What a joy it would be for you to see God's people experience great things happening in their lives because of what you were willing to give!

When we think about the issue of sacrificing for others, we discover that we all pale in comparison to the love and sacrifice Jesus gave and made for us. His demonstration of sacrificial love authenticates and validates His incredible love for you and me. No one has sacrificed more for you than He has, and no one loves you more than He does.

Remember
Sacrifice is an indication of deep love.

Show Choirs

Read

"Fathers, do not embitter your children, or they will become discouraged" (Colossians 3:21 NIV).

Reflect

I remember it like it was yesterday. I have never done it before or since. But on this particular weekend, I drove a thousand miles and spent fourteen hours on the road to hear my daughter sing for twenty minutes at a show choir performance. Being a true dad, I calculated the mileage, my drive time, motel costs, gas costs, and food costs to see this twenty-minute performance. Twenty minutes, that was it! That's two nights in motels, four tanks of gas, a rental car, and eight meals for twenty minutes of singing and dancing. Oh, and by the way, she was great! Here's something else that was strange: I never once thought about all the things I needed to be doing at work or at home. I never thought twice about my undone to-do list that would be glaring at me on Monday morning. Why would I spend so much time, energy, and money to see twenty minutes of show choir competition? It's not because I am into the show choir competition scene, but I am into the Mackenzie scene. Her mom and I are unapologetically Mackenzie fans. We are the same way with her brother, Zac. It is a by-product of being addicted to our kids.

My whole adult life has been about touching a day I will never see. It has been about reaching the next generation with the love of God that changed my life. So when it comes to children, no matter how old they are, I have a soft spot for them. But then so did Jesus. He said, "Let the little children come to me, and do not hinder them, for the kingdom of God belongs to such as these" (Mark 10:14). So when you are helping children, you are really following Jesus's lead and getting a little taste of heaven on earth.

Respond
Showing your children that you support them can be costly; however, not showing them will cost you much more later in life. You create memories just by being involved. What they are doing might not be your thing, but *they* are your thing, and your support is one of the most valuable things you can give them.

Remember
Encouraging your children is priceless. Your kids need your support today.

Surviving a Broken Spirit

Read

"The spirit of a man can endure his sickness, but as for a broken spirit who can bear it" (Proverbs 18:14 NASB)?

Reflect

At one time or another, we all have been the victim of someone's anger. We all have felt attacked by someone close to us. Maybe in the heat of the moment words were said that injured us. We were hurt, and even though the incident is over, we still remember the words. Words can be powerful weapons when used to attack a person, and the scars take a long time to heal. But they can heal through the selfless act of forgiveness.

Solomon made a good point in the above verse. We can get over sickness, and even live with it if we have to, but a broken spirit can destroy us. Vicious words in the heat of an argument can break the spirit of a person.

You've probably heard or been in arguments when the words *never* or *always* were used frequently. These words are deadly, especially when used in anger against children. For example, "You have *always* been trouble to me" or "I *never* wanted you in the first place" are especially harmful statements. They express what is known as an exaggeration. No one *always* or *never* does something. Those exaggerations can cut so deeply that the sound bites of those arguments play over and over in the mind of the one offended to the point that they break the person's spirit.

Respond

Perhaps you have thought about some conflicts you have not resolved. You know that unresolved conflicts do not please God. You have broken someone's spirit. You know what you need to do, but you can't seem to come to the point of doing it. Maybe you need to admit you were wrong, or maybe you just need to forgive. You thought it would go away, but it hasn't—and it won't. Whatever it is, pray that God will help you handle the situation in the way He would.

Maybe your spirit has been broken and your self-image is fragile. Let me assure you that God loves you and there is nothing you can do to make Him stop loving you. Pray that God will help you realize this right now in your innermost being. With His help, not only can you endure, but also your broken spirit can be restored.

Remember

He can heal your broken spirit.

The Faith Must Be Passed On

Read

"And Joshua set up at Gilgal the twelve stones they had taken out of the Jordan. ... He did this so that all the peoples of the earth might know that the hand of the Lord is powerful and so that you might always fear the Lord your God" (Joshua 4:20, 24 NIV).

Reflect

I think sometimes we forget that the God of the past is still God today. He still works in miraculous ways, and He is still intimately concerned about us. The lessons we heard in Sunday school as children are the lessons that help us remember who God is and what He is capable of doing. Those stories remind us that if God can make giants fall at the hands of children, make city walls fall at the sound of trumpets, make hungry lions find praying Christians inedible, make a fiery inferno seem like an air conditioner to the courageous, and even make donkeys talk, then He can handle the problems we face.

God did not have the twelve stones put on the riverbank that day just for Joshua and the Hebrew nation to see. He had them put there for future generations to see how He worked on that day and how He can work in our lives today. He knew that Joshua's generation would have children, and then there would be grandchildren and great-grandchildren who would come to Gilgal. They would walk along the banks of the Jordan River. When they noticed the stones, they might ask, "That's strange. How many stones are there?" "Twelve; one for each tribe of

Israel," Grandpa might reply. Then, with captured attention, the grandkids might ask, "Why?" And with a smile, the old-timer would share the centuries-old account: "So you won't forget the miracle that happened here."

Respond
You don't have to wait to see stones piled up on a riverbank to worship. Neither do you have to wait until the weekend to have a worship time with God. God is at work every day of your life. It is up to you to stop, take notice, and worship Him for His movement in your life. In fact, you can stop right now and praise and thank Him for His personal moves in your life. Now, pray that God would use you to pass on the faith to someone you know.

Remember
Pass on your testimony of faith.

The Fruit of Repentance

Read

"Produce fruit in keeping with repentance. And do not think you can say to yourselves, 'We have Abraham as our father'" (Matthew 3:8–9a NIV).

Reflect

Have you ever had someone do you wrong and, when you confronted him with the offense, been promised that he wouldn't do it again—But then within a few days, you see him repeat the same behavior?

There is probably no greater feeling of despair than that which comes with being betrayed. Yet God feels this every time we sin. That is why repentance is such a big deal to Him—not repentance in word, but in action. John the Baptist said that true repentance is demonstrated by action. He called it "the fruit of repentance." In other words, you can say you're repenting all you want, but unless you produce evidence of repentance, it is unlikely that any change has taken place. The fruit of repentance includes stuff like stopping drinking, stopping doing drugs, stopping the affair you're having, and stopping lying—and the list goes on and on. *Stop!* Then start some new habits. Start forgiving, start loving, and start praying.

The Jews of John's day thought they would go to heaven based on their standing as Jews. But John assured them it wasn't what their ancestors did that made them spiritual; it was only through what Jesus did. When you accept what He did for you, it stimulates a response and produces the fruit of repentance.

The only way to see the fruit of repentance is to follow the discipline of turning away from sin. Has turning away from sin become a habit in your life? Can you recognize sin and turn away from it before you indulge?

Respond

The church of Jesus Christ grew because people recognized their sins and repented of them. They changed and put away their old, sinful habits, replacing them with habits of godliness.

In the stillness of your time alone with God today, ask God to give you the strength and courage to let go of habitual sin and let Him take control of your life. One note of caution: You might not feel like repenting, but do it anyway. Why? Because it's God's will and He always blesses repentance.

Remember

Repent is a verb.

The Hinderers

Read

"A few days later, when Jesus again entered Capernaum, the people heard that he had come home. So many gathered that there was no room left, not even outside the door, and he preached the word to them" (Mark 2:1–2 NIV).

Reflect

I am not a fan of long lines, traffic jams, or crowds. It's not that I'm claustrophobic; I just like to move at will. I like to have the freedom of going where I want to go when I want to go there. Crowds have a way of slowing things down to a snail's pace or even bringing movement to a stop. Have you ever been to a major concert or a sports playoff game? People who make up those crowds are often characterized by limited vision, a negative attitude, and the singular ambition of serving themselves. By trying to see what is going on ahead of them, they miss seeing what needs are present around them. That's what happened on one of the busiest days in Jesus's ministry.

News had spread that Jesus was in Capernaum. He was popular at the time. Stories of the miracles He performed and the teaching He proclaimed spread like wildfire. So when word got out that He was at a friend's house in Capernaum, the crowd gathered to the point that no one could move in or out. Among those who heard of His location were four men who had a friend that was paralyzed.

Respond

The crowd. Let's call them the hinderers. They hinder those in need from getting to Jesus. They are curious about Jesus, but they are characterized by no vision, selfishness, and a negative attitude. They blocked the doorway by trying to see what was going on inside. When the creative friends tore a hole in the roof of the house to lower their paralytic friend down before Jesus, the crowd shouted against the plan. They probably didn't mean to hinder, but they did.

How do you hinder others from coming to Christ? By doing nothing? By standing in the way? By questioning creative progress? Don't be a hinderer. Look around. There are many who have been paralyzed by the world system and who need a touch from the Savior. If only they had a friend to get them to Him!

Remember

The friends who make a difference are not impaired by the crowd. They find the best route to bring help to those they love.

The Second-Chance God

Read

"Then the word of the Lord came to Jonah a second time: 'Go to the great city of Nineveh and proclaim to it the message I give you'" (Jonah 3:1–2 NIV).

Reflect

When my son was a child, he and I played a lot of basketball games with each other, one-on-one. Most of the time I would beat him. But every time I beat him, he usually said, "Let's go again, Dad." He always wanted another shot at me. He wore me out—and I loved it!

Everyone would like a second chance to do better. The great thing is that even though we don't always get a second chance at some things in life, God will give us a second chance. He gave Jonah a second chance after he disobeyed and, consequently, put several people in danger. The reason He gives us a second chance is because He is a loving, forgiving, and merciful God. He wants to see us come to a new place of obedience. He wants to bring us to the point that our lives honor Him totally.

Another reason God gives us a second chance is because of the possibilities of our obedience. God could see the future benefits of Jonah's obedience, so He gave Jonah a second chance to share His message with Nineveh. The second chance resulted in seeing a city of 120,000 people repent. To read about the pagan city's repentance should give us hope today for our own nation and leaders. With God, all things are possible.

Respond

I am not convinced that Jonah was a great orator. It was the God behind the message that made the impact. God's message through Jonah was simple: "Forty more days and Nineveh will be destroyed." God knew that Nineveh would repent if Jonah would go; He just needed a willing servant who would trust Him. Initially, Jonah was not that guy, but God graciously gave him a second chance—and through Jonah's obedience, the culture of an entire city was changed.

It could be that God is giving you a second chance today, a second chance to make something right, a second chance to forgive, a second chance to love, a second chance to obey. Thank God for His willingness to give you a second chance.

Remember

You can give someone a second chance today.

Forgiveness

Read
"But if you do not forgive men their sins, your Father will not forgive your sins" (Matthew 6:15).

Reflect
Several years ago in a small town in northwestern Missouri, two brothers owned a store and were partners in every sense of the word until the day when one of the brothers left a dollar bill on the counter. He turned around, and when he turned back, the dollar was gone. He asked his brother if he had picked it up, but the other brother denied it. An argument ensued, followed by more accusations and denials. This led to other suspicions. The brothers encouraged the townspeople to take sides, and eventually the two brothers broke the partnership. Still wanting to own the business, and with neither of them willing to relocate, they put a line down the middle of the store and competed for business. Some twenty years later, a big car pulled up in front of the store, and a wealthy man got out. He walked into the store and asked to speak to both brothers. Unaware of what had happened to the brothers' partnership, the man confessed to stealing the dollar as a little boy. Years of false accusations and mistrust ruined the relationships of the brothers, their families, and the community. What a price to pay for an unforgiving attitude!

Forgiveness entails canceling punishment. It means to erase what is due, to give up resentment. We are not commanded to forgive when we feel like forgiving. We are commanded to forgive regardless of our feelings. When you are hurting, the last thing you want to do is give up resentment. Families all over the world are characterized by built-up resentment and stored-up grudges. Forgiveness is a necessary step to restore relationships.

Respond

When Jesus died on the cross, He paid the price for all your sins. When you accept the gift of His sacrifice, God the Father cancels your punishment. Two words characterize His forgiveness—*immediate* and *complete.* He does not put conditions on His forgiveness. He never says, "I'll forgive you, but ..." In the same way, Jesus says we must forgive. To refuse to forgive affects you negatively, both emotionally and physically. An unforgiving heart shows. It shows on your face and is revealed in your actions. When you do not forgive, your blood pressure rises and you can become a bitter person. Forgiveness is God's gift *to* you and *for* you.

Remember

If you choose to walk in forgiveness, you will walk with God.

Service

Where you invest your life determines your legacy.

"Whatever you do, work at it with all your heart, as working for the Lord, not for men" (Colossians 3:23 NIV).

A Story to Tell

"Now the Lord provided a huge fish to swallow Jonah, and Jonah was in the belly of the fish three days and three nights" (Jonah 1:17 NIV).

Reflect
Stories are powerful. One of the greatest stories in the Bible is found in the book of Jonah. Most people have read it or at least heard about the great fish that swallowed Jonah. Few believe, but I think James Bartley would have believed it.

James Bartley had a great story to tell. It was 1891, off the coast of the Falkland Islands where James and several other whalers were searching for the next big catch. A large whale was spotted, and the two boats pursued the huge mammal. With hearts pounding and harpoons ready, the whalers zeroed in on their target. When the command was issued, the harpoons began to fly and the whale was struck. In the whale's distress, one of the boats moved too close to the animal. With a flip of the whale's powerful tail, two whalers were thrown overboard. One was found, but he had drowned. The other—James Bartley—wasn't found.

The sailors continued their work of seizing the whale. After they had subdued the huge beast and hauled it to shore, they began to cut away the fat. After two days of dressing the whale, they reached the stomach. What happened next was nothing short of remarkable. Something moved in the stomach. As the men cut gingerly around the form in the stomach, they found their friend James Bartley. He was unconscious but alive. His body was bleached after being dosed with seawater. For two weeks James was treated. He fully recovered with a whale of a story.

Respond

Jonah's experience was even more amazing. He was not in pursuit of a whale. The fish was commissioned to pursue him. He wasn't holding a harpoon, just a rebellious attitude toward God. Jonah wasn't working for his living; he was running from his calling. Two men at sea, two men swallowed by a great sea creature, two men delivered: one with a story to tell, and the other with a mission to complete.

Jonah completed his mission to tell the story of a God, who demands repentance and delivers with grace. The entire city of Nineveh heard the message of the half-digested prophet and repented.

Remember

God is willing to take extreme measures to capture your attention.

Committed to the Dream

Read

"Come, let us rebuild the wall of Jerusalem, and we will no longer be in disgrace" (Nehemiah 2:17b NIV).

Reflect

Martin Luther King Jr. popularized the phrase *I have a dream.* He never saw his dream brought to completion, but he was committed to bringing about change that would lead to his dream becoming a reality. God desires our commitment to the fulfillment of His dreams for our lives.

God is looking for people who are committed to His dreams. His dreams involve reconciling the world to Himself. His dreams involve loving the unlovable and serving those who are unable to return the service. His dreams are consistent with His commands. His dreams center on His agenda of going into the entire world and teaching the same things He taught while He walked on earth.

To understand God's dreams, we must spend time with Him. He reveals His dreams through His Word. When we get into His Word and learn more about Him, we will discover He is not interested in our ideas. He is interested in His ideas being worked out through our lives. It is important to spend time with Him so that we can catch a glimpse of His dreams. Will you consider the commitment necessary to carry out His dreams?

When God selects people to carry out His plan, He chooses those who have no interest in making themselves look good.

Rather, He chooses those who get enjoyment out of honoring Him. Not only did Nehemiah receive enjoyment from pleasing God, but also those leaders who followed him caught his enthusiasm from his appeal to "no longer be in disgrace." The contagious vision of making God respectable in the eyes of the world captured and controlled Nehemiah's heart.

Respond

What are God's dreams for your life? What walls does He want you to rebuild? What venue does He have for you to make Him look good and respectable to the world? Does He have a dream that is capturing and controlling your heart? Let Him search your heart today. Ask Him about your family life and whether you are giving it your best. Ask Him to help you in your work to build walls that will protect you from being influenced by those who ignore God. Ask God to give you the strength and courage to be an influence on those who do not know Him. Finally, ask Him to enhance your commitment to His dreams for your life.

Remember

God wants you to be involved in carrying out His dreams.

The Thrill of Being On His Team

Read
"For we are God's handiwork, created in Christ Jesus to do good works, which God prepared in advance for us to do" (Ephesians 2:10 NIV).

Reflect
I love to see a team turn a double play in baseball. A fast break in basketball that involves no fewer than three passes excites me. I'm off my seat and shouting when a quarterback launches a Hail Mary pass for the win. What do all these sporting feats have in common? Cooperation. Each requires several people working together to achieve a significant goal. The ultimate goal for any team is victory. Teams are fun and exciting. When working in sync, they provide a feeling of encouragement that cannot be produced by one person alone. Most encouraging is knowing that God wants you on His team. He wants you to experience the thrill of cooperating with Him.

Respond
Like most teams, God's team has a common goal—to do His will, "to do good works ... prepared in advance for us to do." To see His will accomplished in your life and on earth thrills Him. Another exciting aspect of God's team is that He is always recruiting. "The eyes of the Lord move to and fro throughout the earth that He may strongly support those whose heart is completely

His" (2 Chronicles 16:9a). He is on a search for hearts that are cooperative with His agenda.

The challenge with many team members is that they sometimes question the coach. Moses was one of those team members. When God shared His plan of delivering the children of Israel from slavery with His key strategy of using Moses as the leader who would direct, inspire, and complete the mission, Moses balked. One excuse after another was thrown back to God. Each excuse was laced with fear. But in the end, Moses cooperated with God and the greatest exodus in history occurred. When Moses cooperated, God demonstrated miracles that only could be explained by the presence and power of His hand moving.

Are you on God's team? Are you cooperating with His agenda, or are you excusing yourself from His plan? What fears are you feeding to excuse your participation in God's plan? The coach can be trusted. The team can be trained. The plan will be accomplished when we cooperate.

Remember
When we cooperate with God, it gets all of heaven's attention. But most of all, He is thrilled.

Don't Let Projects Get in the Way of People

Read
"Each of you should look not only to your own interests, but also to the interests of others" (Philippians 2:4 NIV).

Reflect
Today I was reading through my journal from a few years back. My journal is made up of daily letters to God, usually recapping the day from start to finish. It is fascinating to remember how God speaks to us at certain times in our lives. Hope you enjoy.

> You name it, Lord, and I didn't do it today. I didn't get much of anything accomplished that I had on my to-do list. Too many people were demanding my time. However, I was able to help some of them, so I guess I should look at that as productivity. Wait a minute! If that's the case, I guess Your whole life was productive. Where do I get off thinking helping others is an imposition? Helping others is supposed to be one of the driving forces of my life.

> I stayed up late to meet tomorrow's deadlines. Thought about all those time-management people who say, "If you managed your time better, you'd get more done." They have good ideas, but not a whole lot of people like those ideas. Did You ever struggle with time management? Project management? Guess the whole world was Your project. Did You ever get criticized for withdrawing from people to be by Yourself? Did people

ever call that being unproductive? Forgive me, Lord, for ever looking at the people whom You love and for whom You died as impositions and interruptions. Give me wisdom to handle the difficult ones, courage to correct the wrong ones, and sensitivity to reach out to the hurting ones. Amazing. As I write these words, I remember You love them all just as much as You love me. Their projects are just as important to You as mine, because they are just as important. Thanks for Your productive love. It produces in me that which I cannot produce myself. I love You, Lord.

Respond
How much time are you spending on the interests of others? Are your projects helping others? Just for fun, sit down and write God a letter thanking Him for taking time for you and always having your best interests at heart.

Remember
You are not His project. You are His personal friend.

Equipped to Serve

Read

"So that the servant of God may be thoroughly equipped for every good work" (2 Timothy 3:17 NIV).

Reflect

I have seen young people who were excited about serving God but were not equipped to serve Him. They had the energy but not the knowledge. I have seen others who prided themselves in their Bible knowledge but who would not lift a finger to help someone in need.

The purpose of Bible study is not just to help us understand doctrines or to defend the faith, but to equip us for service. The word *thoroughly* in the verse above means, "to complete in fit shape or fit condition." In other words, the Bible gets us into shape spiritually so we can effectively serve the Lord. If we are to be a people of God, His Word must control us. Just like Moses, Elijah, Elisha, Daniel, Paul, Timothy, and others, we can please God if we make His Word the key influence of our lives.

God's Word not only provides the means of equipping us for service, but it also protects us from involvements that would hurt our service. By allowing God's Word to infiltrate our lives, we will begin to see areas of our involvement that do not please God at all. You may have thought, *I can do this and still serve God effectively.* But you know the truth of His Word, which reveals your need to eliminate that compromising involvement. It may be something that is the noblest of ventures, but if it is something God is not in, you shouldn't be involved in it either. It takes courage and honesty with yourself to choose only those activities and involvements that please Him.

Respond

Are you equipping yourself for service? Do you seek the truth of God's Word daily? Take some time right now to praise and thank God for His Word. Thank Him for the times His Word has helped to comfort or correct you. Now take a moment or two and ask God to reveal your heart to you. Share with Him the times you have failed to follow Him, and ask Him for forgiveness. Finally, pray that both someone you know and you will walk in truth today, no matter what you face. Now, go out equipped to serve Him today.

Remember

We are saved to serve.

Faithful with a Few

"His master said to him, 'Well done, good and faithful slave; you were faithful with a few things, I will put you in charge of many things, enter into the joy of your master'" (Matthew 25:21 NASB).

Reflect

Faithfulness. What a great word. It is a word every employer wants to use to describe his employees. It provides security to the wife whose husband travels and is away from home. It offers hope when one is discouraged. It is what we all need in a friend and what is nonnegotiable for a marriage. It is steadfastness when encircled by stress. It is loyal perseverance when surrounded by pressure. It is not impossible. It has a model: Jesus. He was faithful to what God had called Him to do, and He still is faithful today.

To be faithful to someone or something means you are not distracted from your object of faithfulness to the point of abandoning that person or thing. Your behavior is not altered by circumstances or tough times. You are trustworthy and can be depended upon to do what you have pledged to do.

Of all the things God rewards, faithfulness is at the top of the list. Take the apostle John as an example. He was faithful to Jesus and was known as the disciple whom Jesus loved. He was the only disciple recorded who followed Jesus all the way to the cross. He was the only one who was allowed to look into the future, see the end of all things, and write about it in the book of Revelation.

John was also the only disciple who died of natural causes. If you want to know if it is worth remaining faithful to Jesus, look at the life of John. He demonstrated faithfulness consistently and authentically.

Respond
Being faithful is not something Jesus asks us to do when we get old. In fact, age has nothing to do with it. His desire is that you learn to be faithful now in every area of your life: your relationships, your talents, your time, your money, your possessions—everything! When you practice faithfulness, you will experience a more fulfilling relationship with God.

Remember
When you are faithful with a little, He will trust you with more.

God Is at Work; Join Him

Read

"Jesus said to them, 'My Father is always at his work to this very day, and I, too, am working'" (John 5:17 NIV).

Reflect

Several years ago when my daughter was small, I was in the backyard mowing the lawn with my old push mower. Typically it took about hour to mow. On this particular day, my daughter, Mackenzie, who was five at the time, came outside and wanted to help me. Trying not to be negative, and having a little extra time, I agreed to let her walk in front of me with her hands on the push bar. Even though she thought she was pushing the mower, she was really just hanging on. I, of course, had to slow down to make room for her to walk between the mower and me. The work went more slowly, but it was okay with me because she felt like she was helping. Then after only a few minutes, she began to tell me the manner in which I should mow the lawn. She even pushed me away and said, "No, Daddy, let me do it." At that point I stopped pushing, and guess what? The work stopped. It occurred to me at that point how God works many times with me.

God does not need my help, but He chooses to allow me to play a part in His work. Many times I think He must slow down the process to involve me, but because I am His treasure it doesn't seem to bother Him. He is just glad I have joined Him. But then there are those times when I think I know a better way to accomplish His work. That's when He may take His hand away and stop the work. But if I will just hang on with Him, He will do the work I could never do.

Respond
God is always at work around you. The exciting thing is, He wants you to work with Him. It is up to you to make the choice to join Him in His work. You will be amazed at the things He will accomplish in and around you.

Remember
He is working patiently to produce a result that will be beautiful if you would cooperate.

God Is on a Mission

Read

"For God so loved the world that He gave His one and only Son, that whoever believes in Him shall not perish but have eternal life" (John 3:16 NIV).

Reflect

I have loved the *Mission Impossible* franchise ever since I was a child. For each episode, I was glued to the TV, waiting for the opening line, "Good morning, Mr. Phelps." Mr. Phelps would open an envelope containing an audiotape and pictures of various people, and receive instructions about a secret mission he was to complete. Then the voice on the tape would say, "Your mission, Jim, should you choose to accept it." After laying out the mission, the tape would self-destruct.

Many of you reading this today have seen the *Mission Impossible* movies or remember the TV series. Perhaps you can hear the theme song in your mind. The show was exciting because the mission was exciting. But let me tell you what is really exciting. God is on a mission in this world. His mission? To rescue a world of people who do not know Him personally in order to bring them to a relationship with Him. Our mission as believers is to carry out His plan by reaching out to those we know with His love.

Respond

To carry out His mission, God gave what was most valuable to Him, His Son, Jesus, to reach and reconcile the world to Him. Because sin had entered the world and separated human beings from God, a sacrifice had to be made to pay the penalty for humanity's sin. God, in His mercy, made a way for humankind to be reconciled: through the sacrificial death of His Son.

People can accept or reject the gift of God's Son. Many today ignore God and the sacrifice He made because they are distracted by the world. But that does not change God's mission to reach them. Perhaps you know someone whom you think of as a "mission impossible," someone whom you think will never become a Christian. Let me remind you of something: your mission, should you choose to accept it, is to show that person God's love living through you.

Remember

God's love is your resource to accomplish His mission of reconciling the world.

God's Work Involves You

Read

"For we are God's workmanship, created in Christ Jesus to do good works, which God prepared in advance for us to do" (Ephesians 2:10 NIV).

Reflect

One of my fondest memories is working with my dad on the farm. I cannot honestly say I always enjoyed it, because I was a kid. Kids like to play when there is work to be done. But through his patience, he balanced my play and work in order to properly prepare me for adulthood. When we worked together I was never worried about the work, because he was with me. I simply did what he said and good things happened.

This was true not only with work but also with what my dad loved. He taught me what to love. He loved my mom, so I loved my mom. He taught me how to relate respectfully to adults. He taught me how to treat people, both men and women. He taught me how to engage others and how to know when to be quiet. Working with him shaped my life, making me become who I am today.

God started His work long ago. Because we matter to Him, He wants to work with us, in us, and through us. The truth is, however, that we do not always like the way He works with us. We want to have our own way and follow our agenda. We want our desires to be fulfilled ahead of His work being accomplished. But God is patient and works with us, protecting us until we show signs of becoming cooperative with Him. Then, when we decide to join Him, He gives us responsibilities to carry out His work.

God also works with us on what and whom we should love. He loves all of us, and He wants us to love each other. According to 2 Corinthians 5:20, we are to be His representatives on this earth to spread His message of love.

Respond

The church is His vehicle for spreading His love and doing His work. The stronger the church grows, the more effective God's mission. This means His work involves you and me. The resources He has so graciously given us are to be used for His work. Are you cooperating with Him in His work on planet Earth?

Remember

Your gifts and resources were designed to make Him look good.

He Wants to Receive a Return

Read

"'And I was afraid, and went away and hid your talent in the ground.' ... But his master answered and said to him, 'You wicked, lazy slave, you knew that I reap where I did not sow, and gather where I scattered no seed'" (Matthew 25:25–26 NASB).

Reflect

I am sure the servant Jesus is referring to in today's Scripture was a nice guy. He likely had friends who thought he was pleasant to be around. Socially, he was probably acceptable and had some good personality traits. Yet this servant was not given much, and he proved not to be faithful even with the little he was given. He simply did nothing. The result? He was called wicked and lazy by his master.

What do you have to do to be wicked in the eyes of God? Nothing! It is clear that God expects some things from us. He makes them easily understood. We don't have to wonder what our Master wants from us; we know. He wants us to be faithful with what He has given us. He wants to receive a return for what He has invested in us. Since He invested the life of His own Son, Jesus, it's easy to see what He expects from us—He expects our faithfulness.

God does not want us to be faithful because He is a demanding grouch in the sky. He wants us to be faithful because when we are, we get to know Him better. He is the true prize of faithfulness. We discover His love and resources, and we understand His kingdom thinking, which is incredibly different from the self-centered thinking we experience every day on earth. The blessing of faithfulness is not just that we will be blessed but that we get closer to the One who blesses.

Respond

Our heavenly Master is not unfair with us. He lets us know what it takes to please Him. We never have to guess. So the questions are as follows: Have you been faithful with the gifts He has given you? Have you been faithful in your relationships? Is there any selfishness in your life that would cause you to hold back from giving God your very best? God has been faithful to give us His very best. Today is our opportunity to return the favor.

Remember

Be faithful.

Help Even When It Is Inconvenient for You to Do So

Read

"Late in the afternoon the Twelve came to him and said, 'Send the crowd away so they can go to the surrounding villages and countryside and find food and lodging, because we are in a remote place here'" (Luke 9:12 NIV).

Reflect

He called me on the phone and said, "Hufty [we were on a last-name basis], I need you to go somewhere with me. I will pick you up in five minutes." A member of our church, he had a hard shell on the outside and a marshmallow on the inside. He had three daughters and was on his way to pick me up to go talk to his oldest one. She had run away from home to a drug house located about ten miles from his house. When he stopped by my office, I ran outside, got into his truck, and asked what was going on. He began to explain that she had run away from home and wouldn't listen to him. He said, "She might listen to you, so I need you to go in there and get her out."

My initial thoughts were fearful ones. I had never done drugs, much less even gone into a place where drugs were present. I remember thinking that I hadn't planned my day to go like this. As I entered the house, I heard my friend's daughter crying in one of the back rooms. She was lost, hurting, abandoned by so-called friends, and in need of love. I told her that her parents really loved her and that's why I was there. She listened. She came home. Love worked again.

Respond
Jesus and His disciples had been through a long day. A crowd of over five thousand people surrounded them. To compound the pressure, those people were getting hungry. When the disciples said to Jesus, "Send them away," I don't believe they were not benevolent. I think they were just being practical. I also think they were doing two things we should never do: (1) ridding themselves of any sense of responsibility and (2) telling Jesus what to do. They knew their limitations, but they didn't fully know their Lord. He challenged them to help. With His help, they saw one of the greatest miracles ever performed this side of heaven.

Remember
When it seems inconvenient, look close, because the Lord might be involved.

How Do You Know Where God Is Working?

Read

"As long as it is day, we must do the work of him who sent me. Night is coming, when no one can work" (John 9:4 NIV).

Reflect

God is at work all around you. The challenge comes when you say, "Well, I don't know if God wants me to get involved here or not. I better pray about it." Please understand my heart as I say these words: some things you do not need to stop and pray about; you need to pray as you go. If you already know that some things are God's will, you just need to do them. I have seen many people hesitate and just be a spectator of what God was doing, never getting in on what He was trying to accomplish.

There are some consistent criteria that follow His work. First, when God works, whatever He does will be consistent with Scripture. He will not work outside His Word or contradict it (2 Timothy 3:16–17). Second, He will work in a way that opposes the flesh. He does not wish for any person to get credit for what only He can do (1 Corinthians 1:26–30). More evidence of God working in our lives is that the work He wants to accomplish will require our faith (Hebrews 11:6).

Respond

The question is not one of where is God working as much as it is one of whether or not you will accompany Him in the work He is doing. When we join in His initiatives, we discover many benefits as a result. First, we will see life from a larger perspective. God's work involves more than what we do for Him. He touches more lives than you ever imagined as a result of your obedience to Him. Second, as we work with God on one of His projects, somewhere in the process we will sense that He is not only working with us, but also that He is working in us. At other times we will be amazed that He is working in spite of us.

Can you see where God is working around you? Ask Him to help you be watchful of where He is working around you, and then ask Him to give you courage to join Him.

Remember
God loves to include you in His work.

Influencing Others by Caring for Them

Read

"Joseph, a Levite from Cyprus, whom the apostles called Barnabas (which means Son of Encouragement)" (Acts 4:36 NIV).

Reflect

There is an old saying: "People will never care about what you know until they know that you care." Barnabas was one of those New Testament guys who cared about others. He was known for his compassion. His nickname was "Encourager." He was the kind of guy you like to have around. When things seem to be going south on you, it's great to have a Barnabas-type guy around to lift your spirits.

Barnabas was the one who encouraged Paul in his early years of ministry. Paul took Barnabas with him on some of his mission trips. Paul knew that to go on a mission trip without an encourager could be disheartening. So he found a faithful friend in Barnabas. Barnabas also encouraged his cousin John Mark to continue in the ministry after John Mark had failed on one of those trips. It can be assumed that one of the reasons we have the gospel of Mark today is because of the encouragement of Barnabas.

Encouragers. Don't you love them? People like that earn the right to be heard by others. Since they are willing to listen to others when they are hurting, they are more likely to be heard when they share something of significance. Through this encouragement we can influence others in a way that will be positive and productive. We all need a Barnabas in our lives. But that's not all. We need to become a Barnabas to others.

Respond

Are you a Barnabas-type person? Do you make a point to lift up those who are down, or do you just give people instructions on how to get over a situation and call it encouragement? True encouragers take the time. They are not enablers. They do not drop the standard. They encourage you and let you know you are not alone.

Encouragers are greatly needed in life. They make tough times tolerable and good times wonderful. A key tool used by Satan to weaken believers is discouragement. We need an encourager in our lives to help strengthen us during dark and uncertain days. Who is your Barnabas?

Remember

When you are encouraging, you are dealing a blow to Satan's strategy on earth.

It Is Very Hard to See When
My Eyes Are on Me

Read

"For by the grace given me I say to every one of you: Do not think of yourself more highly than you ought, but rather think of yourself with sober judgment, in accordance with the measure of faith God has given you" (Romans 12:3 NIV).

Reflect

I hope the title of today's devotion caught your eye. It is a line out of an old Keith Green song entitled "Make My Life a Prayer to You." Every time I sing it, this line captures my thoughts and places a conviction in my heart to focus on Him more so than on me. It's very hard to see life from the proper perspective when my comforts, my concerns, my needs, and my desires cloud my vision, leading it away from what He desires. After all, He told us that if we seek Him first, He will take care of all the comforts, concerns, needs, and desires we have. You see, He already is focused on us; therefore, we are free to focus on accomplishing His work.

Paul urges us to get our eyes off ourselves in order to experience real life. Paul had earned the right to say this because of the grace God had given to Him. God rescued him from the ladder-climbing trap in the religious circle of his day. God turned Paul's zeal from persecuting the church to promoting the church. The very ones he was trying to censor were now the ones he was trying to sustain. When he saw the grace of God working in his own life and got his eyes off himself, he turned the world upside down for Christ—and we still talk about it today.

Respond

God has a priority today—you! He sent His Son to the world to reconcile you to Him. He wants you to serve Him in reconciling others to Him. He has a vision for your life. He wants to take the blinders of the world away from your eyes so you can experience all He has for you. Are you willing to get out of the "me first" mentality? Are you willing to place today's cares, concerns, needs, and desires in His hands? Remember: He is already focused on you.

Remember

You can see life better when you focus on the giver of life.

Just Do It

Read
"For whoever does the will of My Father who is in heaven, he is My brother and sister and mother" (Matthew 12:50 NASB).

Reflect
Notice in this verse Jesus said, "For whoever does the will of My Father," not "For whoever *knows* the will of My Father." To know God's will is only half the journey, for only by doing His will can we wholly please Him.

Sometimes we act pretty ignorant to what the will of God is. We may say, "Well, if I knew His will, I would do it." But in reality, we *do* know His will and just don't want to do it. For example, do you know it is God's will for you to have consistent time alone with Him to build your relationship with Him? Do you do it? Do you know it is God's will for you to share your faith with others as He gives you opportunity to do so? Do you do it? Do you know it is God's will that you give a tithe of what He allows you to earn? Do you do it? James explains it this way in James 4:17. "To one who knows the right thing to do, and does not do it, to him it is sin."

But when you do His will, amazing things happen. He reveals to you His will that you do not yet know. That's right. When you do the will of God that you do know, He graciously reveals more of His will to you. When He sees you can be trusted with a little, He will give you more.

Respond

So, how can you please God? Do His will. The New Testament emphasizes not only knowing God's will but also doing it. So we simply need to take what we know and do it. When we make doing His will a daily practice of our lives, we begin to discover other parts of God's will. Just as Jesus said in the parable of the talents, "His master said to him, 'Well done, good and faithful servant! You have been faithful with a few things, I will put you in charge of many things. Come and share your master's happiness'" (Matthew 25:23 NIV)!

Remember

It is not enough to know God's will. Doing His will is the real accomplishment.

Know Your Limitations

Read
"Moses' father-in-law said to him, 'What you are doing is not good'" (Exodus 18:17 ESV).

Reflect
Iconic actor Clint Eastwood has played many challenging roles, none probably more intimidating than his role as Harry Callahan (Dirty Harry), the cop that often colored outside the lines to solve a case. One of his famous lines from his movie *Magnum Force* is, "A man's got to know his limitations." What a great line. Although from an action film that is far from Christian in nature, the line could not be more accurate for a person living the Christian life.

Moses, the one whom God chose to deliver His people from slavery, had many great qualities. He led with conviction, he prayed with passion, and he fought with courage. However, as an administrator he was weak. He took it upon himself to be the judge and jury for all the affairs of his people. His father-in-law saw what he was doing and wisely stated to him, "What you are doing is not good." That's another great line. Jethro, Moses's father-in-law, told Moses he was going to wear himself out by carrying the burdens of the people that he was not expected or designed to carry. He told him not to do a job that was not intended for him to do. Have you ever considered Jethro's advice in relation to what you are doing now?

Respond
Not all noble things are the right things for you. Moses was trying to help settle people's issues, but he thought he was the only one who could do it. Moses's father-in-law was telling him that he was going to wear himself out. People will do that to you. They will drain your energy with their problems and pain. Yes, someone needs to help, but you must know your limitations. You are limited in your ability to help, and to think you are not is prideful.

Some people need to be needed. Guard yourself against being one of those people. We must absolutely help others, but we must also realize when we are hurting ourselves by taking on too much.

Remember
God sent one Savior into the world, and you are *not* Him. When you try to save the world, you drain yourself of energy from aiding those you may truly be able to help.

Lessons from a Powerful Parable

Read

"Therefore take away the talent from him, and give it to the one who has ten talents" (Matthew 25:28 NASB).

Reflect

The story that Jesus told about talents answers a simple question: what do we do until He returns? Like the master in the story, His return will be unannounced and purposeful. He will show up while we are going about our daily activities and will want to know what we did with what He gave us. He has given all of us gifts. We do not all have the same gifts, nor in the same abundance, but we all have the same responsibility. We are to use our gifts. Notice what happened to the servant who was unfaithful in using his gift. The gift was taken away. In simple terms: use it or lose it.

Today we would say someone has talent if he or she can sing, can play an instrument, or is athletic. In the New Testament context, a talent was a monetary unit that was worth about six thousand denarii. A denarius was equal to a day's wage. The man who had five talents had about thirty thousand days' wages. The people who heard this story were probably amazed at the generosity of the master to give such a sizable gift to his servant.

Of the three servants mentioned in the story, two were productive and one was lazy. The servant who buried his gift was afraid of his master. In the end, he lost everything. If you believe that God is harsh and quick to condemn, you might not use what

He has given you for fear you will mess up. This inaccurate view of God actually keeps us from receiving more from Him.

Respond
God looks for servants who are faithful. As soon as the master took away the talent entrusted to the unfaithful servant, he gave it to the one who was faithful. Christ distributes gifts to His servants. If they are faithful to use them, He gives them more.

How faithful are you with what God has given you? When the Master returns, will He find that you have been faithful to use what He has given you to expand His agenda?

Remember
The Master is returning to see what we did with what He gave us.

Making a Big Move

Read

"Now then, you and all these people, get ready to cross the Jordan River into the land I am about to give to them—to the Israelites" (Joshua 1:2).

Reflect

Joshua had his work cut out for him. He faced a big move—actually, several big moves. He had to face the big move of becoming his nation's leader. He had played second fiddle to Moses for a long time and was comfortable in that role. But now Moses was gone and God appointed Joshua to replace him.

Think of the challenge Joshua faced in moving from that comfort zone of his life. Yes, he wanted to obey God, but did God really know what He was doing? Here was Joshua, shielded by the shadow of Moses's leadership for years, preparing to turn his back on the past and to take the challenge of the future. He must have remembered how at the most influential moment of his life, forty years earlier, he failed to convince the people to enter the Promised Land. Would he be successful in convincing them this time?

When we are challenged to move ahead, we often look back and see our failures. However, God doesn't. He knew Joshua had what it took to be the leader of Israel. God didn't throw the past in Joshua's face. He, in essence, told him to forget the past and to move forward.

Respond

Have you received a challenge from God but have been haunted by your past? God wants you to forget the past and focus on who He has groomed you to be. He has erased the past in order for you to move forward with your life as His servant.

Just as God had a plan for Joshua, He has a plan for you. As you consider how God is going to use you in the future, pray this verse as a part of your daily time alone with Him. "Teach me to do your will, for you are my God. May your gracious Spirit lead me forward on a firm footing" (Psalm 143:10 NLT).

Remember

Your past is just that, past. Let it go, and move forward with God's blessing.

Praying and Planning Go Together

Read

"The king said to me, 'What is it you want?' Then I prayed to the God of heaven, and I answered the king, 'If it pleases the king and if your servant has found favor in his sight, let him send me to the city in Judah where my fathers are buried so that I can rebuild it'" (Nehemiah 2:4–5 NIV).

Reflect

When Nehemiah received news that the walls of Jerusalem had been torn down, it broke his heart. He knew that the state of Jerusalem was important to God, so he prayed and planned. He prayed to God for four months. Nothing happened in the first week, the second week, or the tenth week. For sixteen weeks he prayed and nothing happened. But finally, the king noticed him. The king asked Nehemiah, "Why does your face look so sad when you are not ill?" After four months of prayer and planning, the opportunity presented itself.

Here are some of the lessons we can learn from Nehemiah and his success:

1. Before you talk to people about God's work, talk to God about humankind.
2. Before you talk to people about how they can help, talk to God about the abundant provisions He has for you.
3. Before you listen to the opposition, listen to the Father.

As Nehemiah prayed, he planned. God worked in his life not only to give him the vision for what He wanted but also to give him ideas on how to carry it out.

God does not lead us to places where He has not gone before (John 10:4). Just because we face opposition does not mean God has not preceded us on the path. It only means we get to prove to Him that seeing His dream come to pass is important to us. When we face opposition with a focused determination on Him, He blesses our faithfulness.

Respond
Nehemiah was faced with two thrones, the throne of the king and the throne of God. We, too, are faced with two thrones when it comes to our decisions in life. Until we dethrone ourselves and bow before His throne, we will never find the fulfillment of the Christian life.

Remember
Praying and planning go together.

Purses without Holes

Read
"Sell your possessions and give to the poor. Provide purses for yourselves that will not wear out, a treasure in heaven that will not be exhausted, where no thief comes near and no moth destroys. For where your treasure is, there your heart will be also" (Luke 12:33–34 NIV).

Reflect
Jesus taught his followers to sell and give. In doing so, He was teaching them to avoid the greed of this world that destroys. He was also teaching them to develop trust in God that would be forever rewarded. His teaching reminds us that by centering our lives on the treasures of this world, we run the risk of losing everything. But if we store up heavenly treasures, He guarantees us an eternal reward.

In today's verse, Jesus teaches that greed is like carrying around a big purse full of change and never noticing that the change is falling out because the purse is worn out and full of holes. The Bible says if we live a greedy life, we cannot please God. When Jesus tells us to avoid greed, He is trying to protect us from the bondage of being owned by a possession.

Respond
During this teaching session, Jesus said that what you treasure reveals your heart. Where is your treasure? What is it that you treasure more than anything else? That is exactly where your

heart is. Your passion is found in what you treasure. If your treasure is anything material in nature, get ready to lose it. It's an eventual guaranteed loss. But on the other hand, if you treasure a relationship with Christ, you will never lose it or its benefits.

Try to use the two verbs Jesus mentioned in the verse above as a motto for your life and avoid the greed trap. Number one: *sell.* Don't be owned by anything or anyone but Jesus. Number two: *give.* The reason God allows His children to have more than they need is so they can give more away. When you are not owned by possessions and you become a giver, you are demonstrating how to make your number one treasure in life be Jesus.

Remember
Don't be greedy. Be a giver.

The Rewards of Being Trusted

Read

"For to everyone who has, more shall be given, and he will have an abundance; but from the one who does not have, even what he does have shall be taken away" (Matthew 25:29 NASB).

Reflect

We learn so much about God through the parable of the talents. We can learn that He is a generous Master; He gives to each of us differently; and He expects us to be faithful with what He gives. We learn that He will return to receive a report on our progress and that He will not tolerate laziness and unfaithfulness. The Lord reveals Himself to us through this story so we can know Him better and meet His expectations when we see Him again.

Another thing to note from Jesus's story about the talents is that God wants to give us more—not to satisfy our greediness, but to enable us to be faithful with more. The gifts God gives us are designed to make Him look good to those around us. His gifts are a platform for us to produce an appealing view of Him to others. Too often, though, we take His generous gifts and try to make ourselves look good, which is why He doesn't give us more. If we glorify Him with the gifts we have received, He will entrust us with more. That's the way of God.

Respond

Let's take a gift inventory. How trustworthy have you been with the gifts God has given you? Have you used them in a way that would honor Him? Have you taken advantage of opportunities to show others how gracious He has been to you? Are you developing a mind-set of generosity and service that trumps your own selfish desires?

Take a few minutes to praise and thank Him for those gifts. Thank Him for the talents and abilities He has given you, and ask Him to show you how you can be the most effective servant possible with those gifts. When He speaks to your heart as you sincerely seek Him, ask Him to give you the courage to obey His call.

Remember
Your gifts are a platform to make Him look good, that is, to glorify Him.

Lie Down

Read
"Therefore I urge you, brethren, by the mercies of God, to present your bodies a living and holy sacrifice, acceptable to God, which is your spiritual service of worship" (Romans 12:1 NASB).

Reflect
I remember the first time I heard the word. I didn't like the sound of it, and I liked even less what it meant for me. My dad said it to me. I was just about ready to step into the batter's box as a nine-year-old slap hitter. We had a runner on third (my brother) and nobody out. It was a close game. This was my opportunity to be a hero. I wanted to swing away. I wanted to hear the people cheer. However, my dad had a different plan. What I heard was my dad saying, "Tommy, come here." I looked over to the third-base coach's box, and there came my dad walking toward me. He put his arm around me and said it. "I want you to *sacrifice.*" "What do you mean, sacrifice?" I asked. He said, "I don't want you to swing away; I want you to lay down a bunt." Those phrases sounded so opposite. *Swing away.* I loved that phrase. I practiced that all the time. *Lie down* sounded like "take a dive," "give up." But he was firm. "Lay down a bunt so your brother can score. They will get you out, but he will score." I did what my dad said, and his plan worked. I laid one down, my brother came running home, and a member of the opposing team threw me out. I looked and saw my brother sliding in safe at home. If you are a baseball fan, you know that it was a beautiful thing. If you are a nine-year-old who

wants to swing away, you know that to me it felt like a waste. No one expected it. But when your father is the coach and you want to live, you do what he says.

Respond
No one expected the sacrifice more than two thousand years ago. The world was a confusing place back then. The Romans ruled with an iron fist over the Middle East and in Jerusalem. No one was looking for a sacrifice. The Jews sought someone with strength to swing away and deliver the people from Roman rule. Instead, they got a sacrifice—a Savior. The Savior.

Remember
His sacrifice was more than a model; it was a mandate for us to follow.

Serving by Encouraging

Read

"Then we will no longer be infants, tossed back and forth by the waves, and blown here and there by every wind of teaching and by the cunning and craftiness of men in their deceitful scheming. Instead, speaking in truth and love, we will grow to become in every respect the mature body of him who is the head, that is, Christ" (Ephesians 4:14–15 NIV).

Reflect

Not long ago, a young woman who had been in our youth group called me. She was in college and was facing some struggles. Some of her closest friends were introducing her to doctrine she had not learned at home. To her, the doctrine was strange and not biblical. The winds of false teaching were blowing, and she needed some support. Actually, she was more stable than she thought. She asked questions about what Scripture said on a certain subject and then answered them properly without a lot of help from me. But she still needed support to take a stand in the midst of controversy. We all do. When she was convinced her interpretation was correct, she felt a stabilizing strength, but at the same time she felt a sorrow for her friends who had been misled for so long.

No one can blame a baby for acting like a baby. But there comes a time when maturity must develop. Paul illustrates this by using the analogy of waves on the sea. He knew how a boat could be tossed in a storm; he had experienced that firsthand.

In the same way, a believer can be blown away by incorrect doctrine. The results are no direction and no control.

Respond

Are you encouraging anyone in the body of Christ now? We are to build each other up with the gifts God has given us. When we do, they produce maturity in our lives and strengthen the church. Then we can be stable when the winds of discouragement try to blow us around.

How stable are you in God's Word? Are you attracted by things you had never heard before that sound good? Do you measure what you hear with Scripture? Ask God to help you become more and more grounded in His Word.

Remember

You can serve God by encouraging others in their faith.

The Assignment

Read

"Then I heard the voice of the Lord saying, 'Whom shall I send? And who will go for us?' And I said, 'Here am I. Send me'" (Isaiah 6:8 NIV)!

Reflect

I once heard a minister say, "God cares not if the vessel is chipped or cracked, only if it is clean." The truth is, God will use anyone who is cleansed and has repented from his or her sin. So, if we have confessed and repented from our sins, God wants to use us.

After God cleansed and forgave Isaiah of his sin, He gave him an assignment. He asked him two questions: "Whom shall I send? And who will go for us?" God desires to use us to accomplish the work of His kingdom. He has an agenda He desires to accomplish through us if we are willing to embrace His plan. Isaiah willingly volunteered for whatever God desired. In simple terms: God's assignment was for Isaiah to go and teach people everywhere about God's ways, but Isaiah was to realize that when he preached and taught, no one would listen to him.

Isaiah asked the obvious question: "How long [do I have to do this]?" God's answer was, "As long as there are still people to hear it." This response tells us how much God loves people. Even though there are times when people are unwilling to listen to God, He still pursues them with His love, because people matter to God.

Isaiah took God's challenge personally. He did not say, "Here I am; send my friend." He said, "Send me." Our culture is in a state of spiritual decline much like Isaiah's culture was. God is still calling, "Whom shall I send?" How will you respond? I encourage you to willfully say to God, "I'll go where you want me to go and do what you want me to do."

Respond
Like Isaiah, you, when you have an authentic encounter with God, will want to serve Him like never before. You will be so grateful for His blessing and forgiveness in your life that serving Him will be a natural response. Spend some time every day praying for those He has placed in your life. Ask Him to make you a clean vessel and to use you to impact their lives.

Remember
God always has an assignment for us.

Pay It Forward

Read
"Now he who supplies seed to the sower and bread for food will also supply and increase your store of seed and will enlarge the harvest of your righteousness" (2 Corinthians 9:10 NIV).

Reflect
I never left my grandmother's house empty-handed. She always made sure that when I left I had some food or a gift. I used to tease her about it, but she would just say, "I have been given so much, I have to share it."

God gives to us so we can give in turn. Even the salvation He provided for us when Christ died on the cross was intended to come to us on its way to someone else. In other words, we are expected to pass it on. All the benefits, blessings, and resources God gives to us are not supposed to stop with us. God expects us to be a channel of giving.

This helps explain today's verse. God *increases our store of seed*, that is, our ability to bless others, so we can become a storehouse of blessing to others. Now you might say, "But my storehouse is not that big." From all indications from Scripture, the size of the storehouse is not what is in question when it comes to being a giver. What matters is the size of the giver's heart. Today's verse says that God will supply and increase your store of resources so you will be able to enlarge your ability to produce righteousness through giving to others. How much righteousness is being harvested in your life? How much of your life is producing righteous fruit? Remember: enlarging the harvest of your righteousness is one of God's goals for you.

Respond
Spend some time with the Lord, praising Him for His generosity to you. Take some time to thank Him for the "store of seed" He has given you. Thank Him for the faithful relationships in your life. Ask Him to forgive you for the selfish choices you have made when others around you were in need. Finally, pray that He will use you today to be a channel of blessing to someone.

Remember
When you give of your time, talent, or treasure to others, you are imitating what God does for you every day.

The Model of Serving Love

Read

"Your attitude should be the same as that of Christ Jesus: Who, being in very nature God, did not consider equality with God something to be grasped, but made himself nothing, taking the very nature of a servant, being made in human likeness" (Philippians 2:5–7 NIV).

Reflect

Warren Wiersbe tells the story of a successful job counselor who had placed several hundred former applicants in their vocations. When asked about the secret of his success, the counselor replied, "If you want to find out what a worker is really like, don't give them responsibilities give them privileges. Most people can handle responsibilities if you pay them enough. But a real leader will take their privileges and use them to advance the company. Jesus used His privileges for the sake of others" (Warren Wiersbe, *Be Joyful* [Wheaton, IL: Victor, 1974], 60).

No one has ever given up more for you than Jesus has. For Him to be the ruler of the universe in heaven, surrounded by perfection, and to leave it to live among us on earth is nothing short of incredible. His model of love is the epitome of servanthood.

Paul says Jesus did not consider equality with God as something to be grasped. In His humility, Jesus saw sinners as valuable enough for Him to lay aside His place in heaven in order to come to earth and pay the price for sin. Did He know what

He was getting into? Of course. And He still came. That is the ultimate expression of humility and service to others.

Respond
What do you consider worthy to be grasped in your life? Jesus decided to grasp the opportunity to serve others. Through serving, He demonstrated humility and love. Those two attributes were like a magnet to those who followed Him. His followers modeled the same character traits, and so should we today.

Humble yourself before God and praise Him for what He has done for you through Jesus. Ask Him to cleanse you for the times you have sought to grasp things in life that displeased Him. Finally, pray that He will lead you to serve someone and expect nothing in return.

Remember
To serve others is to model what Jesus did.

You Can't Outgive God

Read

"Yet it was good of you to share in my troubles. ... Not that I am looking for a gift, but I am looking for what may be credited to your account" (Philippians 4:14, 17 NIV).

Reflect

Giving is a two-way street. When you give with the correct attitude, it does something inside you. Have you ever given something to a child and seen him or her light up? In fact, when you bought the gift, you were subconsciously thinking about how he or she would respond. And when you gave it, you watched the child explode with joy. Do you remember how great that felt? You couldn't produce that feeling in any other way than by giving.

From prison, Paul explains the principle of giving to the Christians in Philippi. He knew that when they gave, even if it was to him, God would give them a blessing. Why do you think God blesses those who give? I believe the reason is that we are never more like Jesus than when we are giving. His whole life was a gift to us. In the same way, we are to be givers to others.

Respond

If I were to come to your house and take a sledgehammer to your favorite possession, you would probably say, "Tom, you're paying for that." You would be right in your judgment, because I would be indebted to you. In the same way, when we sin, God says, "You're going to pay for that sin." Yet Jesus stepped in and said, "I'll pay for that sin." Therefore, the debt to God has been paid for you and me, not by anything we did, but by what Jesus did for us. That is the ultimate in giving: giving when there is no guarantee of return, giving when others are helpless to pay you back. To imitate Jesus is to become a giver.

Paul said that when you give and serve, it is marked on your account with God. He knows when you are serving and how you are giving. Ask God for opportunities to give of your time and resources to someone in need.

Remember
Serving is an act of giving.

Gotta Serve Somebody

"No one can serve two masters. Either he will hate the one and love the other, or he will be devoted to the one and despise the other. You cannot serve both God and money" (Matthew 6:24 NIV).

Reflect
Bob Dylan wrote a song several years ago titled "Gotta Serve Somebody." Dylan has been a controversial figure over the years, but the lyrics of this song could not be more accurate. The narrative of the song refers to different types of people—some wealthy, some famous, some brilliant. However, they all have one thing in common: they all serve(d) somebody or something. They had to choose whom or what they would serve. One line of the song says, "It may be the Devil or it may be the Lord, but you're gonna have to serve somebody."

In today's verse, Jesus gives the example of serving either God or money. The two are really opposites in what they produce. If you serve money, you will be tempted to become greedy and want more. If you serve God, you will have a tendency to be a giver and give more. Jesus said you cannot be totally devoted to both.

Serving involves much more than lip service. True service requires investment of your time, mental energy, money, and resources. You give of yourself out of dedication to the one you serve. Jesus said He came to this earth to serve. He served all of us as our Savior. Today, He serves us as our advocate to the Father. If we are Christ's followers, we take on the same role of servant to one another.

Respond
Servanthood is a blessing, especially in relationships. It is difficult to criticize someone who is serving you. Whom are you serving today? Are you serving your own interests or the interests of God? Ask Him to help you serve Him in sincerity and truth today. Thank Him for His patience with you and your selfish desires, and ask Him to cleanse you of having been too selfish with what He has given you.

Remember
True service comes from the heart.

Doing Something Significant

Read

"You are the salt of the earth. But if the salt loses its saltiness, how can it be made salty again? It is no longer good for anything, except to be thrown out and trampled by men" (Matthew 5:13 NIV).

Reflect

During biblical times, houses in the Middle East typically had flat roofs. Even today, if you see panoramic video footage of that area, you will notice that flat-rooftop architecture is prevalent.

In Bible times, the roof was an active place for social functions in the Middle East. People would throw parties on the roof, dance on the roof, and hold business and family activities on the roof. The Middle Eastern structure was used in the same way we use our outdoor patios, decks, and porches. The roofs were coated with a tar-like substance called gypsum. Because the roof was subject to so much activity, it would begin to wear and often needed repair. Therefore, additional gypsum was applied to fill the cracks and repair the roof when it was damaged. In order to get the gypsum to coagulate properly, people would oftentimes mix salt with the bitter gypsum to create a durable substance. Jesus said, "If the salt loses its saltiness, how can it be salty again? It is no longer good for anything, except to be thrown out and trampled by men." Jesus is saying that when Christians, who are the salt of the earth, get mixed with the wrong ingredients or find themselves in the wrong environment, they can become weak and are just like that salt: only good to be trampled on by the world.

Respond

One of the most significant things you can do in life is to point someone to the saving power of Jesus. What attracted you to Him? Maybe someone's behavior made you think, *If that's what God is all about, I need Him.* That person probably was not a "secret agent" Christian. He or she probably identified with Christ and was not ashamed, because of what Christ had done for him or her. The person probably was full of joy even though his or her life had challenges just like yours. Do you know why you were attracted to that person? Because he or she was salty and had flavor in his or her life, and you knew you needed what that individual had—something found only through a relationship with Christ.

You can make a significant impact today as you have social contact with the world. When people see you treating others like Jesus would, perhaps they will develop a thirst for God. Pray you will have the opportunity to serve Him by serving others today.

Remember

Salt preserves, creates thirst, and brings out flavor. Be salty today.

Helping People Know God Personally

Read

"We are therefore Christ's ambassadors, as though God were making his appeal through us. We implore you on Christ's behalf: Be reconciled to God" (2 Corinthians 5:20 NIV).

Reflect

As parents, we are always pleased when we hear someone say, "Your son [or daughter] is so well-mannered." We usually smile and wonder if the person saw the right child. But there is a sense of pride when we hear something like that, because all the effort we have put into molding that child's life is somehow paying off in the real world. It makes us feel like good parents because it makes us look good. The same thing is true spiritually. We are to make our heavenly Father look good to the world.

Because we are Christ's ambassadors (representatives) in this world, it is our job to make Him look good to the world. We are ambassadors with a message. The message is that God wants to have a personal relationship with those who do not know Him. Many people think they can only get to heaven by following a set of rules and trying to be "basically good." Our message to them is this: even though that sounds good, it is not true from God's perspective. For if one could get to heaven by being good, then Jesus would not have had to come and pay the penalty for our sins.

Respond

God desires a relationship with us. We do not have to pass a test, because His Son passed the test for us. He has completed the work of reconciliation on the cross to enable us to have a relationship with God. Therefore, we can have a relationship and grow closer to Him daily by spending time with Him in prayer and following His will. His will calls for our involvement in His plan of reconciling the world to Himself.

When others watch you day in and day out, do they think of a loving God living through you? If God is motivating us, we will look for opportunities to serve others and reflect His love. This is a countercultural mind-set, but it can be a life changer for some people who take notice of your behavior. How you live can actually capture the attention of those who do not know God personally.

Remember

You are an ambassador with a message.

CPSIA information can be obtained at www.ICGtesting.com
Printed in the USA
LVOW12s2133290116

472927LV00002B/2/P